Remer

**Personal Memories of Career and Family**

By Jim Peacock

*Renate,
Thank you for your interest and friendship;
Great to have such good neighbors.
Jim Peacock*

# CONTENTS

| | |
|---|---|
| *Copyright* | v |
| *Introduction* | ix |
| 1. My Life Just Happened | 1 |
| 2. Alberta born, a News Beginning | 5 |
| 3. Transition to Journalism | 9 |
| 4. From Jean to Fudsie | 15 |
| 5. Some Highlights and Memorable Points | 19 |
| 6. Edmonton to Toronto to Edmonton to Vancouver to New York in 13 years with CP | 25 |
| 7. Toronto, a Coronation, a Trip to the 1954 British Empire Games and an Interview with a World Champion | 29 |
| 8. New Friends | 35 |
| 9. A Grey Cup, Royal Tour and More Personal Highlights —Ma Murray & That's for Damshur! | 43 |
| 10. Another World's Fair and Royal Encounter | 49 |
| 11. Legislative Reporting and more from CP Vancouver | 53 |
| 12. A Date with Lena Horne | 59 |
| 13. Vancouver to New York Link with Oils on Velvet Painter Joy Caros and a Lifetime of Enjoyment of "Laughing Boy" | 65 |
| 14. Volunteering began in Glenayre | 71 |
| 15. A Great Family Neighborhood | 75 |
| 16. Glenayre years of Fun Celebrations | 79 |
| 17. A Safari, Literally and Figuratively | 85 |
| 18. New York Excitement and Entertainment | 91 |
| 19. My biggest News Assignment | 97 |
| 20. Moving Back to the West Coast | 101 |
| 21. Onion Soup and Another Career Move | 105 |
| 22. A Love Affair with Hawaii | 109 |
| 23. B.C.Telephone Company my first PR client | 115 |
| 24. Sponsorship of Nancy Greene | 121 |
| 25. Mary McLuhan and Teacher Awards | 125 |

| | |
|---|---|
| 26. Variety Club and a new Children's Hospital | 129 |
| 27. MacMillan Bloedel Place and Other Fun Things | 135 |
| 28. A Great Time To Be with MB's PR Team | 141 |
| 29. Party Group was Nicknamed Advertising Old Farts | 149 |
| 30. What The Public Sees Must Be The Real Thing | 151 |
| 31. From Agency to direct BC Tel Employee and Back Again | 159 |
| 32. Naming Science World and Helping to Fund its Development | 163 |
| 33. Energy Development and Aboriginal Relations | 171 |
| 34. Another Energy Project – Hat Creek | 179 |
| 35. Chief Commissioner Connaghan read the Omens Accurately | 185 |
| 36. Five McDonald's at Expo 86 – a Four Month Assignment That Lasted 17 Years | 191 |
| 37. A Post-Expo Trip Down Under | 197 |
| 38. McDonald's Assignment Resumed | 203 |
| 39. More accolades for Ron Marcoux | 209 |
| 40. Wasn't That a Party! | 213 |
| 41. Ron Marcoux Retired after 30 Years | 217 |
| 42. Tunnel Vision and a Warm Relationship with Hans Bentzen | 223 |
| 43. Laurier Institute, Wall & Redekop and Others of Interest | 229 |
| 44. Community Centre Association Volunteers a Fun Assignment | 235 |
| 45. Partisan Politics to help rid us of the NDP | 241 |
| 46. Volunteering to Promote the Arts led to Friendship in Japan | 247 |
| 47. Volunteering Extended to Crossroads Hospice | 251 |
| 48. Ocean Cruising Became a Favourite; We did Twenty | 255 |
| 49. Jean Loved Highway Driving | 263 |
| 50. A Dramatic Turn in Family Life | 269 |
| 51. New Family Health Challenges and a Fateful 2018 Friday | 275 |
| 52. We Remembered a Life Well Lived, Especially the Good Times | 281 |
| 53. Shit My Grandmother Says | 285 |
| 54. Mom was a Lot of Things | 291 |
| Remembering the Good Times | 303 |
| Epilogue | 305 |

Copyright © 2019 by James Peacock

All rights reserved.

No part of this book may be reproduced in any form or by any electronic or mechanical means, including information storage and retrieval systems, without written permission from the author, except for the use of brief quotations in a book review.

ISBN
978-1-9992017-0-8 (print book)
978-1-9992017-1-5 (kindle)
978-1-9992017-2-2 (ePub)

Cover photo credit: Jack DeLorme
Layout & cover design by Crystal Clear Solutions Inc.

*Please note this is a work of nonfiction. No names have been changed, no characters invented, no events fabricated. However, human memories are complicated. This book portrays the truth as the author remembers it.*

# REMEMBER THE GOOD TIMES

# INTRODUCTION

On September 19, 2018, when Virginia, Peggi, Lance and I were at Jean's bedside in Eagle Ridge Hospital, and Kerry was there through a cell phone connection from Philadelphia, Jean gave us a final piece of advice: ***"Remember the Good Times,"*** she said.

That's been my focus in bringing this memoir together – with help from daughters, their spouses, our grandchildren and a host of friends who've reminded me of details, many of which are included to record the names of people whose paths crossed with ours and the activities which brought about those crossings.

I invite you to join me in reminiscing about so many good times in our lives, during which Jean and I were together almost 67 years from our December 15, 1951 wedding date (see cover photo). I've tried to set it all out as accurately as I can. Forgive me if you discover something that's not quite on the factual mark.

# 1

## MY LIFE JUST HAPPENED

Looking back, some unusual, perhaps odd, things had significant influence on my life. Cricket, for example. Onion Soup, for another. Fudge. A colleague's illness played a role, too.

So let's start with Cricket. In a country where hockey news commands much more broadcast time and print space than this somewhat exotic athletic endeavor, cricket triggered a substantial development in my journalism career. It's a longish story. And to understand it, a working knowledge of The Canadian Press at that time is needed.

CP can trace its beginnings to 1910 when, as Canadian Press Ltd., it redistributed news from the Associated Press (AP) to Canadian newspapers, using Morse code and telegraph wires.

The Canadian Press (CP), as the co-operative which became Canada's independent national news agency, was established in 1917 to bring news back from Canadian troops in World War I. Its French language service was inaugurated in 1951; radio broadcast news services were launched in 1954, audio services in the 1960s, and network newscasts in 1979. CP began using the Internet to deliver reports in English in 1997 and added French-language Internet service one year later.

CP now (2019) is a for-profit business, but at the time of my event CP was still a co-operative owned and operated by most of the daily newspapers in Canada. Each member newspaper provided its local news coverage to CP for editing and transmission to other CP members as well as two international news agencies, The Associated Press and Reuters.

In 1949, I managed to get hired by the Calgary Herald as a junior sports reporter. (That, too, has an unusual twist I'll deal with later.) One weekend, an English cricket side visited Calgary to play an exhibition match against a local Canada side. CP needed progressive coverage to satisfy its obligations to the international agency Reuters so Reuters could report the outcome to its clients in England. As a member of CP, The Herald had obligations to provide coverage to CP. So, The Herald assigned its junior sports reporter to the weekend task – me!

I was not well acquainted with the game of Cricket. The Internet didn't exist. I sought out authorities involved with the match to improve my understanding to at least a degree that would enable accurate reporting and learned that Cricket is a team competition played with bats and balls. Each team has eleven players.

The game is set on a cricket field centred on a 20-metre pitch with two wickets each comprising a bail balanced on top of three stumps. A bowler delivers the ball from his end of the pitch towards a batsman at the other end. Armed with a bat made of wood and with a flat-sided blade topped by a cylindrical handle, the batsman protects the wicket and seeks to hit the ball into the field in order to score runs. The ball is a hard leather-seamed spheroid with six rows of stitches attaching its leather shell to the string and cork interior.

Each phase of play is called an innings. In each innings, a batting side tries to score as many runs as possible after striking the ball with the bat. The bowling and fielding side tries to

*Remember the Good Times*

prevent this and dismiss each batter. When the ball directly hits the stumps and dislodges the bails, the batter is bowled (out). When the fielding side catches the ball after it is hit by the bat, but before it hits the ground the batter is out. When ten players have been dismissed, the innings end and the teams swap roles.

Wikipedia says that historically, cricket's origins are uncertain and the earliest definite reference is in south-east England in the middle of the 16th century. It spread globally with the expansion of the British Empire, leading to the first international matches in the second half of the 19th century. The game's governing body is the ICC – International Cricket Council, which has over 100 members. The game's rules are held in a code called the Laws of Cricket which is owned and maintained by Marylebone Cricket Club (MCC) in London.

I can't recall exactly what I filed, by telegraph, to the CP Bureau in Edmonton, but my dispatches caught the attention of John Dauphinee, then Western Editor for CP with responsibility for bureaus in Winnipeg, Edmonton and Vancouver. A few weeks after the cricket weekend, he visited me in Calgary and offered me a job with CP in Edmonton.

I accepted the offer, joined CP in 1951 and worked as part of the CP team for more than 13 years, serving in Edmonton, Toronto, Edmonton, Vancouver and New York bureaus. That whole experience taught me to always try to take advantage of an opportunity to learn something new!

## 2

# ALBERTA BORN, A NEWS BEGINNING

I was born in High River, Alberta, on October 17, 1931, the second son of Arthur and Mary Elizabeth Peacock. We lived in a tiny two-grain-elevator town called Aldersyde and I and my two brothers, Don (for Donald Morris) and Jack (for Robert Jack) and sister, Marion, attended grade school about two kilometres uphill from our house. Aldersyde was a divisional point for the CPR and my father was employed there to help load steam engines with coal and water and to keep engines fired up and ready to go from a roundhouse on the Calgary-Lethbridge rail line. When he advanced to fireman, the family moved to Lethbridge, where I and my siblings attended Fleetwood elementary school and then LCI – Lethbridge Collegiate Institution.

In my first couple of years at LCI, I followed the school's sports teams and sent stories and scores to the Lethbridge Herald, eventually working that into a regular high school news column. I also was involved in newspaper delivery, rising very early six days a week and riding my bicycle to deliver the Calgary Albertan to business and residence customers scattered across Lethbridge. For a time, I also delivered The Lethbridge Herald on an afternoon route.

The Albertan's Lethbridge distribution agent also was its news correspondent. He was virtually blind – and, having heard of my school sports reporting to The Herald, he recruited my help – in return for passes to the games – in covering junior hockey at the Lethbridge Arena. I dutifully filed scoring summaries by telegraph to The Albertan and shared tickets with friends.

My own sports activities were limited. Not by any lack of desire but by religious beliefs held by my Mother. When I was 16, I spent a summer working in a hotel service job obtained in part with the help of a letter from the publisher of The Herald. I was growing exceedingly weary of several church attendances each week. In my own way, I guess I was seeking some kind of personal freedom.

The thought of coming in contact with Presidents, Prime Ministers, royalty and stars of professional sports and the entertainment and artistic communities hadn't entered my head. Nor had the notion of seeing a by-line on articles I had written about the likes of Charles de Gaulle, Lester Pearson, Mickey Mantle and Lena Horne, all of which occurred during a lifetime of experiences that came more by chance and good fortune than by good planning.

My mother was an evangelical Christian who insisted I attend, each Sunday, a morning sermon, afternoon Sunday school and an evening service, plus Wednesday night prayer meetings and an occasional Friday evening missionary visit. Since playing hockey, or any other sport on a Sunday, attending movies, live theatre or a teen dance were all sinful activities, I didn't participate openly in such events.

When that summer came to a conclusion, I chose an alternate route to get out of the family home – enrolling for grade 12 — with strong parental approval, and much to the chagrin of principal D.S.A. Kyle of Lethbridge Collegiate Institute — in a residential high school at Caronport, Saskatchewan run by the religious sect to which my Mother adhered. I had a couple of rebellious teens alongside me there – and we didn't hesitate to

*Remember the Good Times*

break the school rules on frequent occasion. Which led to expulsion and to my being on my own soon after. I have long since recognized that I made a mistake enrolling there, but it triggered another significant turn in my life.

Long before completing my first term at Caronport, my schooling ended. Not before learning, from a riding-the-rails experience, that dumb actions can bring big trouble for you and unintended consequences for innocent parties. Trains fascinated me from a very young age, perhaps because my father worked much of his life for the Canadian Pacific Railway and as a youngster I sometimes rode passenger trains on an employee's dependent pass.

Once, as part of my rebellion against my own Caronport decision, I put his job in jeopardy. Not on purpose but out of ignorance. With a couple of friends, I climbed in a boxcar and rode between two towns, hobo style. Had I been caught and identified, my father could have been fired. And I certainly would have impaired any chance of me being a CPR employee.

As it turned out, I escaped with nothing more than a deserved lecture from my Dad who told me clearly what the consequences could have been. Not too long after that, he helped me find a job with the CPR as a watchman at the roundhouse in Frank, Alberta – famous as the site of a huge landslide.

Like my father at Aldersyde, as a "watchman" I operated a coal shuttle to refuel the steam locomotives of the day and "kept the steam up" overnight on the engines that were kept at the Frank roundhouse while crews slept. My dad progressed to fireman on the engine crew, then to driving the locomotive as a railway engineer (later called engineman). On a couple of Frank Pusher trips, in which the locomotive hitched on to the front end of long freight trains to help haul them over the hills from Frank to Pincher Creek, he was the driver in charge, with me as his fireman.

It's worth noting the Frank slide history here: Wikipedia records that at 4:10 a.m. on Aug. 29, 1903 more than 82 million tonnes of limestone rock slid down Turtle Mountain within 100 seconds, obliterating the Canadian Pacific Railway line and the coal mine located there. It was one of the largest landslides in Canadian history and remains the deadliest. Between 70 and 90 of Frank's residents were killed, most of whom remain buried in the rubble.

The railway was repaired within three weeks and the mine was quickly reopened. The section of town closest to the mountain was relocated in 1911 amid fears that another slide was possible. The town's population nearly doubled its pre-slide population by 1906 but dwindled after the mine closed permanently in 1917.

The community now is part of the Municipality of Crowsnest Pass, Alberta and has a population of around 200. The site of the disaster, which remains nearly unchanged since the slide, became a popular tourist destination, was designated as a Provincial Heritage Site and is home to an interpretive centre that receives more than 100,000 visitors annually.

## 3

# TRANSITION TO JOURNALISM

My work for CPR lasted a few months and included some wild rides as a fireman on the deck of a hand-fired 600-class steam engine used in this case to help pull heavy freight trains over a hill from Bow Island, Alberta towards Medicine Hat, then backed up the 10 kilometre distance to Bow Island to await the next train.

The 600 class engines burned coal to generate steam. The coal had to be shoveled from tender to boiler while standing on a some-times bucking engine deck where each click of the wheels on the rails could be felt. On my "Bow Island Pusher" assignment, my Engineman was a Second World War soldier returned to work for the CPR with his seniority intact – a free spirit with no apparent concern for safety. I don't remember his name, but on one occasion, as I struggled to keep my feet on the bouncing deck of the engine speeding in reverse, I walked over to him and quietly shouted: "Where the Hell is the fire?" He slowed down then, accepting my argument that a pebble on the rails could throw us off the track.

All the exercise involved in shoveling the coal and keeping

my feet to stay upright put me in the best physical shape of my life but soon after the on-board incident over undue speed, I decided a change was in order.

*Jim Peacock, writer-editor-communications counsel in journalism and media relations careers*

I MOVED to journalism in 1949, in part through what turned out to be a fateful letter of recommendation I had requested and received from the then publisher of the Lethbridge Herald, Hugh Buchanan. I sought that letter to help get summer employment at the Prince of Wales Hotel at Waterton Lakes, a popular summer vacation destination in Southern Alberta.

I kept the letter – and when I decided to give up railroading, I took it with me to an interview with Bob Mamini, then Sports

Editor of the Calgary Herald. That experience taught me the value of retaining useful documents. And Bob Mamini, who died far too early in his 40s, taught me much more about the news business, how to build a story with a lead paragraph that delivered the key news element, plus hints of what else was to come if you kept on reading.

IN MY TIME with the Calgary Herald, I also learned about figure skating. The 1951 North American Championships brought some of the world's leading competitors to the city, including Richard Button and Sonia Klopfer. Button was the Gold Medallist from the 1948 Winter Olympics when he came to Calgary, where he won the North American event. During his spectacular career he claimed seven consecutive U.S. championships, the first at age 16, won five World titles and back-to-back gold medals at the Winter Olympics before retiring from competition in 1952. Elected to the World Figure Skating Hall of Fame in 1976, Button remained in his sport's headlines as a prominent television analyst.

Klopfer also won in Calgary. She had earned silver at the 1950 and gold at the 1951 U.S. Championships. She finished third in the 1951 World Championships, fourth in the 1952 Oslo Winter Olympics and second at that year's World's in Paris. With her husband Canadian figure skater Peter Dunfield, she took up coaching. Her students included Dorothy Hamill of the U.S. and Canadian Elizabeth Manley, both of whom became national champions and Olympic medallists.

Organizers of the North American event in Calgary recruited me to help publicize it, my first media relations experience. I prepared news announcements and delivered them to print and radio broadcast media in the city (TV came later).

As a rookie on the sports department staff, I was assigned to cover minor hockey at the junior level, curling and often pro wrestling. There I watched from ringside as little old ladies sometimes tried to interfere with the likes of fan hero Whipper Billy Watson and fan villain Al (Mr. Murder) Mills who were working a circuit that included Calgary, Edmonton and Great Falls, Montana. As a part of the promoter's publicity efforts, he'd have his wrestlers visit The Herald's sports department virtually every week to chat about their upcoming "fights", outcomes of which were predictable if you followed what prompted increased attendance. One night the hero won; another the villain.

Rookies didn't get assigned to main coverage of the city's major sports but I became a fan of the Stampeders football team, which had won the Grey Cup final in Toronto in 1948. Calgary defeated the Ottawa Rough Riders 12-7 before a crowd of 20,013 at Varsity Stadium in the days when a converted touchdown in Canadian Football counted, if converted, six points – five for the TD, one for the convert. That changed in 1958 when the Canadian Football League (CFL) began its formal existence and set its own rules without outside interference. Since then, a TD has been six points, with the option to go for a one-point convert (kick) or a two-pointer (run or pass).

THE 1948 GREY Cup remains one of the most notable games in history, in part because it marked only the second time a Western team had won the Cup – Winnipeg won in three much earlier years 1935, 1939 and 1941. But the biggest impact came from the Calgary fans who travelled by rail to Toronto and turned the event into Grey Cup week with tireless partying in downtown Toronto.

The fan fun and games featured cowboys, chuckwagons, pancake breakfasts on the steps of City Hall and the infamous appearance of a horse in the lobby of the Royal York Hotel. Those Calgary folks, most sporting the big white Stetson hats associated with the Calgary Stampede and the impact cattle ranching had on that Western city's history, started what became an annual Grey Cup Festival.

*Remember the Good Times*

As a privileged member of the press, I became acquainted with such local heroes as Hall of Famer Normie Kwong, doing several interviews over time as he succeeded as a fullback with the Stampeders, went on to play for the rival Edmonton Eskimos, developed business interests and started a family in Vancouver, and eventually became Lieutenant-Governor of Alberta.

## 4

# FROM JEAN TO FUDSIE

Coincidences continued to impact my life. My closest friend during high school was a tall, good looking fellow named Ted Scott. He came to Calgary to visit and introduced me to a beautiful young woman he had met during a visit to Waterton Lakes Resort. Her name: Dorothy Jean Hembree. She went by Jean, was a football fan, (or at least a fan of players like the handsome Greeks Rod Pantages and Pete Thodos of the Stampeders) enjoyed parties and attended a number at the residence I shared with a couple of other Calgary Herald employees, reporter Jim Senter and photographer Jack DeLorme, who took the photos displayed on the cover and on Page 19.

*Ted Scott introduced Jim to Jean*

JIM PEACOCK

. . .

ON SOME OCCASIONS, dressing warmly to attend a Stampeder game was a good idea because of the weather – and it had side benefits. Jean's fluffy fur coat had large sleeves, into which a bottle of rum fit nicely so she and her companions could soak up the warmth of its contents. Fun. All of this led to a wedding proposal and a marriage on December 15, 1951— over the objections of my Mother, whose religious bigotry led to highly unfair treatment of Jean at the wedding and beyond.

Often in our conversations at parties and other events we shared, if something went awry, Jean would say "Oh, Fudge." Rather than the four-letter version, which she also used on occasion in later years. In any event, this phrase and her love of the taste of chocolate fudge led me to call her "Fudsie", which became, for both of us, an affectionate nickname that remained in use right to the end.

It was reinforced by an oversized valentine she gave me early in our life together. Its cover had an image of a fudge-coated cartoon figure and the words "To make sure you'd be my valentine, I had myself dipped in hot fudge". Inside it read: "I know you'd never turn down a chocolate-covered nut. Happy Valentine's Day!" It was signed "love & kisses, Fudsie". The card was saved, the date it was given wasn't.

*The Fudsie Valentine*

*Remember the Good Times*

. . .

I HAD ACCEPTED the CP job offer before then and moved to Edmonton. There I had the good fortune to have another superb mentor — Bureau Chief Don Gilbert, whose ability to impart knowledge of the ins and outs of news writing and editing proved to be invaluable in my progress with CP. His wife Virginia was a most delightful woman and our hostess more than once at dinners and other social functions at the Gilbert residence. Jean and I grew very fond of the Gilberts.

After our move to Edmonton following a short honeymoon visit to Banff and the remote Sunshine Village ski lodge, reached in those days only via a tracked snow vehicle, we began our life together in a tiny basement suite in southeast Edmonton. The house was owned by Ches Roper and his wife Winnie, brother and sister-in-law of Elmer E. Roper, then the CCF party leader in Alberta and later Edmonton's Mayor. That family connection seemed to have no political impact on Ches and Winnie. We never heard a political word from them. They treated us very well as we lived in close quarters and with their support we survived an icy winter during which there were 40 days and 40 nights of minus-40 Fahrenheit temperatures.

Looking back, what a life together ours has been! Not without highs and lows, any and all of the latter without doubt, my fault. But in large part because of Jean's patience, tolerance and determination we survived it all through almost 67 years of marriage and with Jean's advice, wisdom and support for them outstanding over the years, our three daughters matured into highly successful individuals each giving us many, many reasons to be proud of them.

In our early years of marriage, Jean and I often had a private chuckle about people who thought our wedding was of the "shotgun" variety, forced by pregnancy. We married in December 1951. Our first child, Virginia Marion, was born in Edmonton on July 17, 1957— a rather long gestation period?

That was during our second Edmonton sojourn, after time in the Toronto headquarters of CP and before our move in November 1958 to Vancouver. My CP years took us from Edmonton to Toronto in 1953; Toronto to Edmonton in 1955; Edmonton to Vancouver in 1958 and Vancouver to New York City at the end of 1962. Each of those assignments had career highlights and memorable points in our life together.

# 5
# SOME HIGHLIGHTS AND MEMORABLE POINTS

*Jean & Jim courtship embrace*

JIM PEACOCK

Following my 15 years in journalism, I moved on to the practice of media and public relations, mixing many hours of volunteer activities with my work. Over the years, I was privileged to enjoy many career and personal highlights, among them:

1. Marrying Jean.

2. Including in my journalism career an assignment to Washington D.C. to cover the aftermath of the assassination of President John F. Kennedy, the biggest story I covered in 15 years of news reporting and editing.

*Life Magazine back cover photo, Jim is among those in the group between drive-way and White House*

3. Naming Science World British Columbia and helping raise the funds to convert the geodesic Expo Centre to that purpose.

4. Prompting decisions to build a new Children's Hospital on Oak Street in Vancouver after residents had waited more than 15 years for promises to be delivered.

5. Starting a golf tournament in August 1992 at the Arbutus Ridge Golf Club on Vancouver Island that has generated substantial funds for Ronald McDonald House, including a record $127,000 at the 26th consecutive tourney staged August 17, 2018 at the Bear Mountain Golf Club in Greater Victoria.

6. Supervising construction and operation of MacMillan Bloedel Place as part of the Van Dusen Botanical Gardens and meeting W.J. Van Dusen at its opening ceremony, where I assisted him as he used a red hot branding iron to burn the MacMillan Bloedel M logo into a large cedar log at the building's entrance.

JIM PEACOCK

*W.J. Van Dusen, with help from Jim, brands MacMillan Bloedel Place*

7. Serving as the first elected president of the Port Moody Foundation and helping to raise funds towards city hall, library and recreation complex enhancements.

8. Travelling in 1992 with Port Moody Mayor David Driscoll and City Administrator Les Harrington to Zimbabwe, getting Kariba a $10,000 Variety International grant to put a tourist bus on the road and raising more than $10,000 in Port Moody to develop a playing field in Kariba.

9. Helping major enterprises from Canada and Japan negotiate a deal with a First Nation to build a liquefied natural gas export terminal at Grassy Point, near the Lax Kwa'alam community of Port Simpson, just north of Prince Rupert.

10. Negotiating a contract that put Olympic and world ski champion Nancy Greene on the BC Tel team for a short period after her retirement from competitive skiing.

*Remember the Good Times*

11. Handling a news conference, with the help of our youngest daughter Peggi, on Jan. 22, 1991 for **Benazir Bhutto, former President of Pakistan** during her visit to Vancouver for a World Affairs dinner sponsored by The Junior League of Vancouver and Science World; and handling media relations for a visit to Science World by the **former President of the Soviet Union Mikhail Gorbachev** as part of his attendance at the March 27, 1993 Science World Mikhail Gorbachev Dinner.

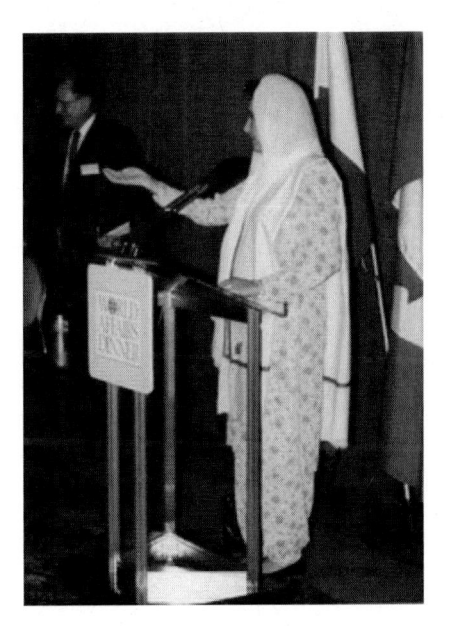

*Benazir Bhutto hands off to Jim at news conference*

12. Helping Charles J. (Chuck) Connaghan with communications related to his role as the first Chief Commissioner of the B.C. Treaty Commission, established by the Federal and B.C. governments to negotiate treaties with B.C.'s many First Nations.

13. Receiving from Deputy Premier Christy Clark, in 2002, the Queen Elizabeth II Golden Jubilee Medal, awarded in Canada to nominees who contributed to public life.

JIM PEACOCK

*Deputy Premier Christy Clark and Coquitlam Mayor Richard Stewart
present Queen's Medal*

More about those later.

## 6

## EDMONTON TO TORONTO TO EDMONTON TO VANCOUVER TO NEW YORK IN 13 YEARS WITH CP

As noted earlier, Jean and I married soon after I began working for CP in Edmonton and it happened in spite of a suggestion from Gillis Purcell, then the head of CP, that marrying might have some negative impact on my opportunities to move around in the CP network since it could impact ease and costs of moving.

That may account for the fact that, while in the first Edmonton stay, I suggested a move to Vancouver would be welcome – and we were transferred to Toronto. There, I suggested a New York posting might be nice. We had no children at that time. Our next posting was back to Edmonton. Vancouver and New York did follow, the former being timely and welcomed, the latter not so much, even though exciting.

Starting our life together in Edmonton, we settled into our meagre accommodations in the Roper basement. We got better acquainted with CP colleagues, attending functions at the residence of the Bureau Chief. I was in awe at the courage Jean showed in her insistence that we return the favour, something her mother, Lottie, had taught her was the right and polite thing to do. We invited Don and Virginia Gilbert to our humble home and they graciously accepted. We helped them find their way down narrow stairs and past a furnace to our living space. Not certain if memory is accurate, but I think we served manhattans before a dinner of beef stroganoff.

My assignments with CP included coverage of home games of the Edmonton Eskimos of the Canadian Football League and the Edmonton Flyers of the Western Hockey League; coverage of both professional and amateur golf, including a national women's amateur championship in Saskatoon in 1951 where I became acquainted with the winner, Marlene Stewart, later adding her married name, Streit. She went on to win the Canadian title ten more times, as well as the U.S., British and Australia titles on her way to becoming the first Canadian elected to the World Golf Hall of Fame.

In a totally unrelated experience many years later I was privileged to meet another famous female Canadian golfer named Brooke Henderson. She had just won the Cambria LPGA tournament in Portland, Oregon at age 17 and was taking part in the 2015 Canadian Women's Open at the Vancouver Golf Club in Coquitlam where I was a volunteer.

She, her father and other aides were waiting outside the press tent for interviews about her becoming an LPGA member even though she hadn't reached the mandated age of 18. I asked if I could take a photo and one member of her group borrowed my camera and snapped a photo of the two of us. A print is among my treasured souvenirs. Brooke went on to win the 2018 CP Canadian Women's Open, played in Regina, the first Canadian to do so in 45 years.

*LPGA golfer Brooke Henderson with Jim*

Regina also figured in my journalism learning processes during my early days with CP in Edmonton. My editing and writing abilities were tested and honed in handling much of the CP coverage of an outbreak in February 1952 near Regina of BSE – bovine spongiform encephalopathy – more commonly known as foot-and-mouth or mad cow disease.

The seriousness of it is reflected in the fact that the U.S. and several provinces closed their borders to livestock imports from Saskatchewan. Major livestock shows and cattle sales were cancelled. Quarantines were imposed and more than 1,500 cattle were destroyed.

The Canadian government moved quickly to contain it and, on August 19, 1952, officially declared the epidemic over. Import bans were lifted and livestock owners were compensated for losses that exceeded $14 million. CP's senior editors expressed thanks to me for my work on that long-running story.

Apparently, in a situation that caused huge concern to families through many agricultural communities impacted by the consequences of the disease, I had maintained a sense of calm objectivity in the language and style of CP coverage of a story with huge potential to cause public panic.

The experience helped me to understand the importance of being objective, sticking to facts and being as accurate as possible in reporting on events I covered. And I had many interesting assignments during my two Edmonton postings.

## 7

## TORONTO, A CORONATION, A TRIP TO THE 1954 BRITISH EMPIRE GAMES AND AN INTERVIEW WITH A WORLD CHAMPION

The first departure from Edmonton took place in 1953 with our transfer to Toronto where we moved into a small apartment in a house in time to watch the telecast from Westminster Abbey of the June 2 Coronation of Queen Elizabeth II. We viewed it on a black and white TV set in the home of our landlords. It was the first Coronation ceremony ever to be telecast and news reports at the time said more than 27 million in Britain watched, along with millions more around the world.

I didn't know it at the time, but I was to have several additional encounters with the Royal Family, including three weeks covering the Western leg of the 1959 Royal Tour of Canada by Queen Elizabeth and her husband, Prince Philip, and a 1962 visit to Seattle to report on the activities of the Prince. The Royal Tour of 1959 also marked the start of a long friendship with National Film Board photographer Gar Lunney, at that time an Ottawa neighbor of my brother Don.

MUCH EARLIER, while assigned to the Toronto CP bureau, I was sent to Vancouver as part of the CP team covering the 1954 British

Empire Games, held in the then new Empire Stadium. The highlight of these games was its "Miracle Mile" in which world record holder John Landy of Australia was pitted against Roger Bannister of England.

Both broke the four-minute barrier, Bannister winning in 3:58.8. Landy finished in 3:59.6. I was in the infield when the race was run and watched with pride as Canada's Rich Ferguson finished third in 4:04.6. I also watched and shared the pain with everyone in the stadium as England's Jim Peters, at that time the world's best marathon runner, entered the stadium with a 17-minute lead, then staggered and collapsed from exhaustion and never did cross the finish line.

Among other highlights of these games was the upset gold medal victory by the UBC-Vancouver Rowing Club men's eights, defeating the favored England team by 10 seconds in a time of 6:59. Vancouver's Doug Hepburn took gold and Montreal's Dave Baillie won silver in men's heavyweight weight lifting; Canada's 4 x 100 relay team won the country's only track and field gold medal; Chris Chataway of England won the three-mile run; and Emmanuel Ifeajuna of Nigeria became the first black African athlete to win an Empire Games gold medal, taking the high jump.

In September, 1954, I was back in the CP Toronto Bureau when a 16-year-old from the city made an historic 21-hour swim from Youngstown, New York to Toronto, crossing Lake Ontario to great fanfare. My September 10th report started: "Marilyn Bell is queen – 150,000 persons said so tonight." It went on to report that at least 50,000 cheered her along the Canadian National Exhibition waterfront, another 25,000 were at the CNE bandstand, 20,000 more at the grandstand and thousands more along the route.

THAT WAS ONLY one of many exciting assignments that brought me in touch with outstanding athletes involved in a wide variety of sports in locations across the country. And it came just ahead of a brief visit Jean and I paid to New York City where we visited Don and Virginia Gilbert and I was able to watch a New York Giants-Cleveland Indians World Series game from a press row seat at the Polo Grounds.

One of the athletes I interviewed back in Toronto was fighter Jimmy McLarnin. The March 10, 1955 Ottawa Journal carried my article:

*By Jim Peacock*

TORONTO (CP) -Somewhere between a dollar and $60,000, Jimmy McLarnin decided there was no romance in fighting. Today he preaches that belief. "The fight game is just for the money," says the Irish-Canadian who once held the world welterweight championship. "Boxing is too tough a game for anything else."

McLarnin, now 47, and prosperous California businessman, spent 19 years in professional fighting, amassing a fortune in ring winnings – and holding on to it to retire wealthy at the age of 29. In 1950, 14 years after he retired, he was voted Canada's outstanding boxer of the half century.

He got his boxing start early, fighting professionally the first time when he was 10 years old, he recalled in an interview during a visit here. "I got a dollar a fight when I was a kid in Vancouver," he said. "It was supposed to be for car fare but I considered myself a paid professional."

Those early preliminary bouts in Vancouver started McLarnin on a long and successful career that took him through 110 fights, including bouts against 14 world champions. He twice won and lost the world welterweight crown, retiring in 1936 after whipping world lightweight champion Lou Ambers in a non-title fight.

McLarnin was born in Belfast, Ireland December 19, 1907. He came to Canada with his parents two years later, settling in Mortlach, Sask., near Moose Jaw. When he was nine, he moved to Vancouver, there becoming a newsboy and making his start in boxing. His fight career began in earnest when he was 13. That was when he met Charlie (Pop) Foster, an ex-fighter who was to become McLarnin's trainer, manager, guardian, counselor and friend.

"I used to work out at a little athletic club in Vancouver," McLarnin said. "Pop came in there now and then and one day he started giving me some pointers. That's how we met." Foster put McLarnin through three years of training and prelim bouts in Vancouver, then one day said "Jim, you're ready." McLarnin was 16. Foster took him south to San Francisco where he fought for promoter Frankie Sands in four-round preliminaries, winning 12 of his 13 bouts and fighting a draw in the other. In 1925, McLarnin got his first main-event fight, defeating Fidel La Barba, then world flyweight, in a non-title match. Jimmy weighed 114 pounds.

From there he campaigned across the United States, appearing in Chicago and finally New York. He met and defeated such world champions as Pancho Villa, Kid Kaplan, Sid Terris, Sammy Mandell, Al Swinger, Lou Ambers, Bud Taylor, young Jack Thompson, Jackie Fields, Benny Leonard and Tony Canzoneri. Sallow-cheeked McLarnin, known across Canada as Baby Face, fought for the welterweight championship in Los Angeles on May 29,1933 against Young Corbett III. He won the match and the crown with a knockout at 2:37 of the first round, the shortest championship battle in the history of the division.

*Remember the Good Times*

One day less than a year later, McLarnin made his first title defence, losing to lightweight champion Barney Ross in New York. He scaled the heights again September 17, 1934, taking a 15-round decision over Ross to regain the crown. But in the rubber match May 28, 1935 – when McLarnin drew $60,000, his largest purse – he dropped the title for good, losing again to Ross in 15 rounds in Los Angeles.

He fought three times after that, twice meeting welterweight champion Tony Canzoneri, who took over when Ross grew out of the division, and lightweight Lou Ambers once. He lost his first fight with Canzoneri, but reversed the decision October 25, 1936. His last fight was in November 1936, a month before his 30$^{th}$ birthday, and he defeated Ambers in a non-title bout.

"After that fight," McLarnin said, "Pop Foster told me: 'Jim, you've got a good bank account, you've got your health, you've had enough.' So I retired. I never doubted Pop Foster's decisions." McLarnin, owner of a travel agency in Los Angeles, in 1935 married Lillian Grace Cupit, a Vancouver school teacher, and they have four children – Ellen, 16, Jean 12, Nancy 7, and James Joseph, 11 months. The McLarnins live in Glendale, a Los Angeles suburb, about a mile from Pop Foster, now 81.

Foster taught Jimmy how to handle his money. "Of course," Jimmy says, "there was quite a bit of difference in income tax between those days when I fought and now." He said a fighter could take in $100,000 then and pay out only about $7,000 in income tax. Today, he said, nearly half of it would go to tax.

## 8

## NEW FRIENDS

COVERING STORMS, THE SPACE AGE START AND POLITICS

While we were in Toronto, Jean worked in a secretarial post for an investment firm. A colleague was Kay Walton and through their friendship we met Kay's husband Murray, then other members of her family, including sister Ann and her husband, Dr. Douglas Courtemanche. We were invited to visit a lakeside residence owned by Ann and Kay's parents — Bert and Mary Douse whose home we also visited in Toronto. We tried water skiing and enjoyed picnics, wine and convivial conversations.

Later, the Waltons, the Courtemanches and the Peacocks all resided in Vancouver where we frequently got together at each other's homes, as well over dinner and other outings. Murray was in the office supplies business, as was Jean's brother David Hembree who with his wife Edith became part of this social circle.

Dr. Courtemanche became one of Canada's leading plastic surgeons and eventually had both Jean and me as patients. My problem was relatively minor, removal of a small growth on my right hand that took a few hours of my time in Vancouver General Hospital. For Jean, the issue was much more serious –

breast cancer in the mid 1980s, which is covered in more detail later.

*Kay & Murray Walton at a Toronto lunch*

Our friendship with Kay and Murray continued to the end and included several lunches in Toronto after they returned there and we travelled to that city to see Kerry or to join her for travel to other exotic places, including the Galapogos Islands. Ann and Douglas stayed in Vancouver following Doug's retirement from his medical practice and we continued to meet until we reached the stage where driving the distances between Port Moody and Vancouver became too much for all of us. Ann and Jean stayed in close touch by phone right to the end of Jean's life and I have maintained contact since then.

AMONG MAJOR NEWS occurrences during my Toronto CP assignment was Hurricane Hazel, the most famous hurricane in Canada's history. It swept into Southern Ontario on October 15, 1954, pounded the Toronto region with winds up to 110 kilometres an hour and saw 285 millimetres of rain fall in 48 hours. The damage was immense, with 81 deaths and an estimated $100 million in losses such as bridge collapses, street washouts, and homes washed into Lake Ontario. The Toronto landscape was changed forever.

Most of my work during Hurricane Hazel took place in the safety of the CP offices on University Avenue in downtown Toronto, where I was recording and editing copy filed by reporters on the front lines of the scenes taking place.

In my recollection of that natural catastrophe, none of the vast news coverage at the time mentioned the phrases "Climate Change" or "Global Warning". Those came to life after the Soviet Union started the space age with the October 1957 launch of "Sputnik", the world's first satellite, and after ensuing communications satellites were tapped for weather research.

I had the good fortune to be a witness to that start of the Space Age just a couple of years after our 1955 return to Edmonton. In early October, 1957, two colleagues and I drove north and east from Edmonton to watch a tiny round light pass overhead across clear night skies. The trip followed the launch of Sputnik, the Russian word for "satellite." Sputnik was launched at 10:29 p.m. Moscow time on Oct. 4, 1957 from the Tyuratam launch base in the Kazakh Republic.

It had a diameter of about 55 centimetres and weighed 83.5 kilograms and circled Earth once every hour and 36 minutes. Traveling at 30,000 kilometres an hour, its elliptical orbit had an apogee (farthest point from Earth) of 940 kms and a perigee (nearest point) of 230 kms. Visible with binoculars before sunrise or after sunset, Sputnik transmitted radio signals back to Earth strong enough to be picked up by amateur radio operators. Those in the United States with access to such equipment tuned in and listened in awe as the beeping Soviet spacecraft passed over America several times a day until January 1958, when its orbit deteriorated, as expected, and the spacecraft burned up in the atmosphere.

• • •

DURING THIS SECOND stop at the CP Edmonton bureau, I had several assignments involving politics – election campaigns and election outcomes among them. One involved coverage of both campaigning and voting day results of the Federal General Election of June 10, 1957. I followed M.J. Coldwell, reporting on his campaign stops in Alberta and Saskatchewan. He served from 1942 until 1960 as national leader of the CCF, predecessor in today's New Democratic Party (NDP) and was the Member of Parliament for the Saskatchewan riding of Rosetown-Biggar from 1935 to 1958. Signage outside one of the communities in that riding read "New York is Big But This is Biggar."

Jean travelled with me on some of that assignment and after getting my reports filed we'd chat over dinner about some of the CCF leader's speech contents. Neither of us was convinced by those comments that this was a political party we'd ever like to see in power as Canada's national government. On voting day, thousands of others demonstrated that they also were not socialist or leftist inclined. The Progressive Conservatives, led by John Diefenbaker, won 111 of the 265 seats in the House of Commons in the June 10, 1957 vote, giving them a minority government as they ousted the Liberals and Prime Minister Louis St. Laurent. That minority government survived only five months and a new national election was called for March 31, 1958.

I was involved again in coverage of campaigning and listened to, recorded and transcribed notes and tapes of some Diefenbaker speeches. He was an orator, often inspirational and more often than not in my experience did not complete a sentence or a paragraph. But he touched the hot buttons of most voters, as the outcome proved. On the night of the vote, I wrote from the CP election desk in Edmonton. My brother Don, who also worked for CP for several years, was lead writer that night on the Toronto election desk. I have a copy of the front page of the Lethbridge Herald of April 1, 1958 in which the lead article carried his byline under the headlines: Canada Swept By Tory Avalanche; Liberals, CCF and SC obliterated. He wrote:

"A coast-to-coast avalanche of Progressive Conservative votes has swept Prime Minister John Diefenbaker and his followers into the most lopsided election victory in the 91 years since Confederation."

My byline appeared under these headings: Gunlock Winner; Southern Alberta Rejects Socreds; West Vote Upset I wrote:

"The Progressive Conservatives, their cry for a return to a two-party Parliament and their plea for a stronger mandate heeded, crushed all opposition in Monday's general election. As the party rode to an unprecedented victory, it won 66 of the 72 seats in the four Western provinces and the North, wiped out Social Credit representation and left only five CCFers and one Liberal with their hides."

Later in 1968, my several involvements with British royalty was expanded when Princess Margaret, the younger sister of Queen Elizabeth II, visited Saskatchewan. I was assigned to report on her travels with Prime Minister Diefenbaker through his home riding of Prince Albert and the northern Saskatchewan resort community of Waskesiu and have among my keep-sakes a black and white news photo in which I am clearly in view with the Princess and the Prime Minister. That preceded our move to the West Coast, as did two memorable sports writers events at the fabled Macdonald Hotel in Edmonton.

JIM PEACOCK

Princess Margaret, flanked by the couple whose farm she visited. The photographer captured Prime Minister Diefenbaker on the right and Jim on the left

Since I often covered sports for CP, I became a member of the *Edmonton Sportswriters and Sportscasters Association.* At its first annual Sportsmen's Dinner held May 6, 1957. Guest speakers included Montreal Canadien Maurice Richard. My program from that dinner bears his autograph and the signatures of Eskimo running back Rollie Miles and two-time Canadian curling champion skip Matt Baldwin.

The second Sportsman's Dinner April 30, 1958, raised funds for the Edmonton Cerebral Palsy Association and honored the Edmonton Eskimos as the 1954, 1955 and 1956 Grey Cup Football champions, the first Western team in the modern CFL to win successive Grey Cups.

It was the era of Jackie Parker, Johnny Bright, Normie Kwong and Rollie Miles and they were among the honorees in attendance. It also was an era when CFL players who came to Canada from the U.S. to play in the CFL stayed in the communities to work in the offseason. Bright and Miles were teachers in Edmonton. As a member of the Sportswriters Association, I was able to join them, Parker and others from the Eskimos in a Sportsmen's Curling League where we competed in fun once a week.

OUR FIRST DAUGHTER, Virginia, was born in Edmonton on July 17, 1957. (Incidentally, our Grandson, James Bryce Balcom, also was born in Edmonton, which prompted Jean to drive from the West Coast to Edmonton. When Bryce's sister Keegan Jean was born July 31, 1991 no long drive was needed. She arrived at the then new B.C. Children's Hospital in Vancouver with which I had a close connection through Variety Club work, as described later.)

Soon after Virginia was born, Jean and I purchased our first house, one of the first homes built in the Edmonton suburb of Sherwood Park. We managed a down payment putting together some limited savings, a small grant from a government housing program and several hundred dollars from the sale of beef cattle Jean owned as a legacy of her childhood years living on a ranch west of the tiny Alberta town of Stavely. Sale of that Sherwood Park house when we were transferred to CP's Vancouver office in November 1958 enabled us to make a down payment on a $14,500 house in the developing Glenayre subdivision in Port Moody, a small city about 25 km east of downtown Vancouver.

## 9

# A GREY CUP, ROYAL TOUR AND MORE PERSONAL HIGHLIGHTS—MA MURRAY & THAT'S FOR DAMSHUR!

Our move to Vancouver in 1958 came just in time for me to be a part of the CP coverage of the 46$^{th}$ Grey Cup game, played in Empire Stadium on November 29 before a crowd of 36,567 and won by Winnipeg Blue Bombers 35-28 over Hamilton Tiger Cats. It was the first Grey Cup game under the aegis of the present-day CFL. It also was one of a half-dozen Grey Cup games where I was a part of the CP teams involved in game coverage and the whoopla that surround these events. On occasion, Vancouver showed its worst side in this whoopla – and during the run-up to this game, some of the city's or visiting idiots threw matresses from windows high up in the Hotel Vancouver to the sidewalk on Georgia Street, narrowly missing passers by.

The most memorable Grey Cup for me perhaps was the December 1962 fog bowl between the Winnipeg Blue Bombers and the Hamilton Tiger-Cats at the lakefront Canadian National Exhibition Stadium in Toronto. The Bombers won 28-27 in a game that was spread over two days.

I reported:

"The fog-bound Grey Cup football game, first ever played as a serial, was completed Sunday in the absence of several hundred visiting fans who couldn't wait here for the second chapter of Winnipeg Blue Bombers fourth victory in six years. Several thousand others abandoned the football stadium for radio and television reports of the last nine minutes and 29 seconds of the game, called Saturday because of fog. The defending champion Bombers, playing before an estimated 15,000 of the 32,655 who showed up for the start of the action Saturday, held off the Hamilton Tiger-Cats and won 28-27. The score was unchanged from Saturday. . . the stadium was completely clear Sunday."

There were many career and personal highlights during our time on the West Coast. One with both career and personal implications came in 1959. I was one of two CP staff reporters assigned to cover the three weeks of the Royal Tour of Canada by Queen Elizabeth II and Prince Philip as they crossed the Western provinces and the Yukon. The other was Dave McIntosh of CP's Ottawa bureau.

We reported on the tour and its many stops from Calgary to Vancouver, throughout British Columbia, to Whitehorse and Dawson City in the Yukon, back through Alberta, Saskatchewan and Manitoba to Winnipeg, riding the Royal Train with world press, making new friends and acquaintances – all of this was exciting. But perhaps even better was the opportunity to spend a night at home with Jean. We'd been apart for about ten days. The Royals were touring Greater Vancouver. We were into renewing our acquaintance while we had the opportu-

*Prince Philip, a local mayor, Queen Elizabeth, photographed as Jim looked on from just behind the Queen*

nity. Nine months later, on March 25, 1960, a personal event with life-long impact occurred with the birth of our second daughter, Kerry Ann.

The Royal Tour built many memories and, by sheer coincidence decades later, led to renewal of a friendship, also with long-lasting consequences. Gar Lunney covered the Royal Tour as a photo journalist for Canada's National Film Board. Gar and I became fairly well acquainted during the tour, which included an end-of-train-trip party in the press car of the train in which we were among many sharing a drink with Prince Philip and the Queen's Ladies in Waiting.

Gar had a hand in that event's happening. He'd covered many other Royal events and the Prince knew him well. After whistle stops in several Saskatchewan towns and villages where Brownies turned up en masse to welcome the Royals, they visited one community where there were no Brownies. The Prince yelled to Gar "Where are the Brownies?" Gar reported this to fellow journalists who then dispatched couriers to purchase Brownie-style caps for the media folks to wear in greeting the Royal party that evening when Elizabeth and Philip would spend their last night aboard the train in Regina's rail yards. A Boy Scout hat for the Prince and a Brownie mix for the Queen also were acquired as gifts from the press.

As it turned out, the Queen did not attend the party. My CP partner Dave McIntosh had reported a couple of days earlier that he'd learned in Whitehorse that the Queen was pregnant, a report which brought Dave criticism from many in the British Press, who pooh-poohed the suggestion – which turned out to be true.

The Prince attended the party, quaffed a couple of glasses of Scotch, donned his gift hat and appeared to enjoy the Brownie's theme. The Queen's Ladies in Waiting also enjoyed their quaffs well into the night and reports had it they had difficulty staying awake during the driving through a very hot Winnipeg the following day. I know I had trouble staying awake on that day, too, but for me it was the end of the assignment so, last report written, I was able to sleep all the way back to Vancouver aboard a regular CP Rail passenger train.

I learned years later that Gar had moved to Vancouver and I saw some of his work in local media, including the magazine Beautiful British Columbia. But we had not been in touch until, April 2007 when Jean and I took a 17-day cruise from Vancouver to Hawaii and return. When the ship stopped at Hilo, we decided to stay aboard, enjoy an almost-empty swimming pool and relax in the sunshine. There was one man in the pool with us, his wife sunning in a poolside deck chair. We had been talking about the ship's pilot coming aboard to guide the Zaandam into Hilo Harbour when the man hanging on to the pool's ladder began to describe an experience he'd had – as a photo journalist – covering a Pilot boarding a freighter in stormy Juan de Fuca Strait off Victoria.

I thought there was something familiar about him. I said: You were a photo journalist? He said "Yes." With the National Film Board? He said "Yes." Is your name Gar? He said "Yes." Gar Lunney? He said "Yes." Jim Peacock, we worked together on the 1959 Royal Tour.

*Gar and Anne Lunney*

*Remember the Good Times*

With that, the memories came back. Gar introduced Jean and me to Anne (pronounced Anna), who he often called his Danish sweetheart. While still based in Ottawa, in 1969 he met Anne Grete while on assignment in Montreal. They moved in together and lived in Vancouver where they were married. The four of us met several times during the balance of that Zaandam cruise, then visited often at each other's residences until Gar died March 23, 2016 at the age of 96. Anne remained a close friend of both of us and was personally very supportive following our family's loss of Jean on September 19, 2018.

## 10

# ANOTHER WORLD'S FAIR AND ROYAL ENCOUNTER

Another Royal encounter came in June 1962, when CP sent me to Seattle to cover a visit by Prince Philip, who toured the site of the World's Fair then taking place. He visited the Canada Pavilion, among other stops on the Seattle Fair's site and addressed a formal dinner staged by the English-Speaking Union. Having invested in a tuxedo, which I wore to the dinner, I was able to move among the guests as one of them, without being singled out as media. The following article was published in the June 2, 1962 Victoria Daily Times under the heading "Philip Sets Fast Pace at World's Fair — Reporters, Officials huff along behind"

*By Jim Peacock*

SEATTLE (CP) - Prince Philip continues his Seattle visit today with a tour of the University of Washington and an aircraft plant, in the wake of a fast-paced visit to the world's fair in which he set crowds cheering and had the fair's president exhausted. "I know one thing about him," said Joseph E. Gandy, Century 21

JIM PEACOCK

president, after escorting the Prince for several hours. "When he wants to go somewhere he damned well goes there."

That was the tone of the Duke of Edinburgh's four-hour visit to the world's fair grounds during which he frequently departed from the planned schedule – to the chagrin of reporters, photographers and policemen.

Refreshed after a four-day rest at an interior British Columbia ranch retreat, the Prince landed his personal aircraft at Boeing Airfield where 350 persons met him. Throughout a day that included the whirlwind tour of the fair, a cruise on Lake Washington and Puget Sound and a formal black-tie dinner that continued until after midnight, he appeared fresh and relaxed.

He kept his hosts laughing through visits to the Canadian, British, European and Indian pavilions, the $10,000,000 United States science exhibit, the 600-foot-high space needle and the monorail. The only time the Prince seemed displeased came when he was asked to make a speech before several thousand fairgoers. Indicating he was taken a bit by surprise, he said: "I have been told for some extraordinary reason to say something to you. You're much better to go and see the exhibits yourselves. I hope you enjoy them as much as I did. And a very good day to you all."

At a formal dinner staged by the English-Speaking Union, he told 600 guests: "Worship at the altar of progress is an increasingly popular manifestation but it should not blind people to the need to keep progress in all its forms under control. In particular, I believe that we should concern ourselves that progress does not displace nature indiscriminately."

The Prince, coming to Seattle as a side trip to his visit to Canada for his Second Commonwealth Conference, piloted his Heron aircraft into Boeing Airfield a half hour before noon. He and his party flew directly from Kamloops, near where they had spent the last four days fishing, riding and relaxing.

He was whisked in an open convertible to the fair and stood bareheaded to wave to the thousands gathered to cheer him outside the British pavilion. Everywhere he went thousands of fairgoers – cameras popping – crowded about him. The Prince seemed to enjoy his little side trips – to the industrial pavilion, the coliseum, an outdoor fountain, the monorail which he rode downtown and back, and the spacearium at the science exhibit where he spent 20 minutes taking a simulated ride among the stars.

He kept his time schedule by walking at such a brisk pace that many following him were puffing. Today he is to tour the University of Washington and visit the Boeing Aircraft Company plant here before leaving at 2:30 p.m. PDT for Vancouver. There he rejoins delegates to his study conference.

## 11

# LEGISLATIVE REPORTING AND MORE FROM CP VANCOUVER

During my time in CP's Vancouver Bureau, I became CP's legislative reporter, travelling to Victoria each week from our home in the Vancouver suburb of Port Moody, by car and ferry, when the Legislature was in session. I reported on throne speeches, budgets, debates and legislation as it was introduced and wrote about the personalities holding office, including Premier W.A.C. Bennett, Liberal Gordon Gibson Sr., a successful lumber baron known as the "Bull of the Woods" and David Barrett, who became NDP leader and was Premier from 1972 to 1975. (On occasion, I boasted that when Mr. Barrett arrived at the legislature after being elected MLA, I showed him where the MLA's men's washroom was located!)

Among those who were part of the Press Gallery at the time was Paddy Sherman of The Province, a mountain climber who was one of those who found a Trans-Canada Air Lines Plane that had crashed on Mount Slesse near Chilliwack on December 9, 1956, killing all 62 aboard, including five pro football players from the Saskatchewan Roughriders and Winnipeg Blue Bombers. In 1966, Paddy wrote the book "Bennett" describing the

JIM PEACOCK

long reign of W.A.C. Bennett as B.C. Premier. Paddy signed my copy with this note:

"To Jean & Jim Peacock who understand better than most the problems of finding out just what makes Wacky tick."

Paddy was legislative reporter and columnist from 1960 to 1965, when he was appointed Editor of The Province. He and his wife, Maureen, became friends of ours during our mutual time in the Press Gallery in Victoria.

*Legislative press gallery members, including Jim back row fourth from the left and Paddy Sherman, two more to the right. News was written on the old style Underwood typewriters.*

Every now and then, Jean would find it possible to join me in Victoria and, as a result of one of those visits, another event with life-long consequences took place. On October 27, 1962 daughter Peggi Jean joined the family weeks before we boarded a train to Calgary for Christmas with Jean's family, then to Toronto and then by car on to a posting at the beginning of 1963 with CP in the New York City bureau.

*Remember the Good Times*

Covering the B.C. Legislature during the long premiership of W.A.C. Bennett had many highlights. Bennett was Premier of British Columbia from 1952 to 1972. His government nationalized the B.C. Electric Company in 1961 when that company opposed his efforts to develop Peace and Columbia River power developments. He merged it with the B.C. Power Commission to form B.C. Hydro and Power Authority. I covered much of that development and the controversy surrounding both the original Peace River and Columbia River Treaty power projects that for decades have given British Columbia a huge clean energy advantage.

Bennett's government was in controversy as well in 1958 when coastal ferry service was interrupted by a strike. *Bennett announced the provincial government's take-over of the system then operated by the CPR and the Black Ball Line. That was the start of B.C. Ferries and I contributed to coverage of that ongoing story.

When Bennett hosted a meeting of provincial Premiers at his residence in Kelowna I covered the event for CP, meeting many of the Premiers of Canada's other provinces.

ON ANOTHER OCCASION, I spent a couple of weeks on a driving trip to the north and northeast regions of British Columbia, seeking feature stories in a variety of communities – Prince George, Dawson Creek and Fort St. John among them. In Fort St. John I sought out the editor of the local weekly newspaper to discuss story possibilities. Her name was Ma Murray, already a character known for her spicy wit, her backcountry wisdom and earthy style. She and her husband were founders of the Bridge River-Lillooet News and later of the Alaska Highway News in Fort St. John. In both newspapers she signed her editorials with the phase "And that's for damshur!".

Ma was born Margaret Theresa Lally in Kansas City, Missouri, in 1988. In 2017, in a series of profiles to mark Canada's 150th birthday, Stephen Hume wrote in The Vancouver Sun:

## JIM PEACOCK

"Her adventurous spirit bloomed early. She slipped notes into saddles bound for Alberta ranches from the factory where she worked. Lonely cowboys wrote back.

"She decided to head north and snag one. But she ran out of money, took a job bookkeeping for The Chinook, a weekly paper, and wound up marrying its dreamy, impractical publisher, George Matheson Murray, who would later spend two years as managing editor of The Vancouver Sun.

When boom times in Vancouver went bust, the family moved to Lillooet. He was elected an MLA and she took over the paper. Cantankerous, infuriating, colloquial, vulgar, even racist in the vernacular of her times, she dispensed such earthy wisdom as: 'Government is like your underwear — it smells pretty bad if you don't change it.'

"She published The Alaska Highway News in Fort St. John, then returned to Lillooet where she died at the age of 94 on Sept. 25, 1982. Her secret to a long life? 'A little bit of loving, a little bit of drinking, and a little bit of working — and make damned sure you don't slip on a banana peel and break your hip.'"

On our dinner visit in Fort St. John we talked about things impacting the Peace River Region's economy – extension of the Pacific Great Eastern Railway, oil and natural gas developments and highway improvements, as well as the contribution agriculture made to the Murrays' enjoyment of life.

I had the good fortune in following years to meet Ma Murray several times in more social settings, including gatherings of the B.C. and Yukon Community Newspapers Association and the Canadian Weekly Newspapers Association. She illustrated that she did, indeed live by those elements of her secret to long life.

I remember chatting with her in the lobby of the Banff Springs Hotel on the final day of a national association meeting I was covering for The Canadian Press. "Jim," she said, or words to that effect. "you've got to help me kill this mickey of rye. I can't take an open bottle of liquor in my car." Yes. We found a place, two glasses and got the job done. Fun. And that's for damshur!

## 12

## A DATE WITH LENA HORNE

Another of the interesting people I kept encountering in Vancouver was Ben Kopelow – actor, promoter, agent and a superb organizer of special events involving performers. As a CP reporter, I met Ben many times in his role as publicist for The Cave, a theatre restaurant in downtown Vancouver where famous singers and dancers performed.

The Cave was officially opened in 1937. By the time I was meeting some of its performers, it was owned and operated by Ken Stauffer and his nephew, Bob Mitten. Its licence was for 600 people but it often crammed in 1,000 to see and hear the likes of Johnny Cash, Ray Charles, Tony Bennett, Louis Armstrong, Robert Goulet, Fats Domino, Ella Fitzgerald, Bette Middler, Ike and Tina Turner, Liza Minelli and Mitzi Gaynor. It also supported many local performers, including a large house band led by saxophonist Fraser McPherson.

Thanks to Ben Kopelow and the owners, I interviewed Lena Horne during a rehearsal for one of her performances there. Jean and I dined with Nancy Sinatra at a balcony table and watched as she chewed her fingernails in anxiety while her boyfriend singer

JIM PEACOCK

Tommy Sands performed. I shared a ringside table with Ben and Marie McDonald one evening and watched a table of hockey pros, including one named Billy MacNeil, I knew from my coverage of the Western Hockey League, look on in apparent astonishment to see this reporter sitting there while the glamorous Miss McDonald was introduced as the upcoming act opening on The Cave stage the following evening.

FROM MY LENA HORNE INTERVIEW, I wrote; – as published July 19, 1962 in the Victoria Daily Times under the heading 'I Never Was One to Attract Teen-Age Audience' Says Lena"

*By Jim Peacock*

VANCOUVER (CP) - Lena Horne, her bangs tucked beneath a Little League baseball cap and her slim, shapely figure disguised by a loosely hung cardigan, was musing at rehearsal about night club audiences.

"They've been pretty consistent for me," she said, recalling 22 years of performing in cabarets around the world.

"It started as a single in café society in New York in 1940 and even in those days—let's see, my kids were still babies — I seemed to sing to a more adult audience. "In the trade we call it a whisky and wine crowd. I don't mean to be fresh. It just means they don't drink much straight coke. I never was one to attract a teen-age audience."

From across the room at the Cave Theatre Restaurant where she was working here, Miss Horne might have been a teen-ager herself. The blue baseball cap, white cardigan, flat-heeled shoes, eye glasses and beige slims she wore offered a sharp contrast to

*Remember the Good Times*

the skin-tight sari that wrapped her elegant figure the night before when she kept an audience of 600 so attentive you could hear a whisper.

In either costume, the 45-year-old Miss Horne showed no visible signs of those many years or of the cares of raising two children, Gail, now 25, and Tommy, 22.

Miss Horne, who works cabarets and hotel "rooms" about 22 weeks a year with conductor-husband Lenny Hayton and her own trio of musicians, said she's selfish about the places she works.

"I'm more likely to take much less money to work some place I like," she said, explaining that she limits her appearances to spots like the Coconut Grove in Hollywood, the Waldorf in New York, the Fairmont in San Francisco and The Sands in Las Vegas. Asked how the Cave falls in with this impressive company on her list, Miss Horne said: " I worked here years ago (it was 12 years ago) and they treated me kindly. I like it here. I like the room. When I become familiar with a room, it's like a pair of old shoes or a sweater. It's comfortable."

FOOTNOTE; The Cave Supper Club was located at 626 Hornby Street. It closed in 1981, was demolished and the site saw a parking garage and TD bank open there.

DURING MY PUBLIC RELATIONS CAREER, I also worked with Ben on some fun events which I summed up in notes remembering our friendship prepared for Ben's 90th birthday celebration:

Dear Ben:

## JIM PEACOCK

It's July 10, 2017 and you're celebrating the big 90! Where did all those years go. So fast. So many fond memories. Seems to have started for you and me back in the days of The Cave. We met from time to time to set up this guy from The Canadian Press for interviews with performers showing up at this night club you did so much to promote.

My fondest memory of those was the 30 minutes I spent with the magical Lena Horne who said she included The Cave in her performing itinerary because when she worked there they (including one Ben Kopelow) "treated me kindly . . . I like the room. . . it's comfortable."

Another favorite memory was sitting at balcony ringside table with Jean and Nancy Sinatra watching Tommy Sands perform while his girl Nancy chewed her fingernails in nervous reaction. I also remember a couple of pro hockey acquaintances reacting with some awe when they saw me at a stage-side table with the famous Marie (The Body) McDonald, set up by Ben.

*Ben, Jean and Jim at Richardson celebration*

Jean and I still get pleasure from a photo reminding us of an anniversary dinner at the Hotel Vancouver where BC Tel

*Remember the Good Times*

President Ernie Richardson and his bride, Marion, danced to the live music of Mart Kenny, whose radio hits of the past had been a background to their courtship.

Of course, the fun memories include many lunch hours entertaining passers-by with live performances by local musicians scheduled and organized by Ben Kopelow on sunny days in the MacMillan Bloedel Plaza on Georgia Street. (Being the producer-cum-impresario was great fun! Thanks Ben.)

A few other events brought us together for a while. Then a hiatus. Then a chance meeting at intermission during a Tony Bennett show at the Orpheum – and many visits with you and Dolly followed.

*Dolly, Ben and Jean at lunch*

JIM PEACOCK

Four six-inch-square paintings with the Kopelow signature hang on a wall in our condo as a delightful regular reminder of a long and wonderful friendship. Hope your memories are equally good! Jean joins me in wishing you a Happy Birthday, Ben. Ninety Years. Wow!

## 13

## VANCOUVER TO NEW YORK LINK WITH OILS ON VELVET PAINTER JOY CAROS AND A LIFETIME OF ENJOYMENT OF "LAUGHING BOY"

Vancouver has had many unique characters over time and as a reporter I was privileged to meet a few, among them an artist named Joy Caros who startled some of her neighbors when she hung nudes on velvet on her backyard clothes line while they dried.

In 2019, as I write this, hanging on the wall of my retirement residence bedroom is "Laughing Boy", a happy reminder of an early news story I wrote after arriving on the West Coast to join the Vancouver Bureau of The Canadian Press. It is a painting of the face of a Hawaiian boy done in oils on black velvet by Caros.

I met Joy at her southeast Vancouver home in early 1962. An article for CP, dated January 24, 1962, noted that her artwork, alive with realism, was often scorned by surrealist art fanciers. She couldn't care less. "If the artist can't explain what he's doing then how can we understand it? Most of it (modern abstract art) is covering up bad drawing. When I see a painting, I don't like to wonder what it is. I like to enjoy the feeling."

JIM PEACOCK

*Joy Caros & a nude - oils on velvet*

At the time, as one of few artists working with oils on black velvet, she was earning a comfortable living from the sale of six or seven original works per week. She said she'd been offered much more to reveal the secrets of her success with this technique than for any painting. It's an ancient art that had been resurrected by an American, Edgar Leeteg, then living in Tahiti where he did portraits of Tahitians, including nudes. His fame and the value of his works soared after he died in a 1953 motorcycle accident.

Caros was born in Trail, B.C. and raised in Vancouver and at the time we met was married to a Vancouver policeman and mother of a girl, 9, and a boy, 5. She had begun painting full time five years earlier. "I was doing portraits in pastels. With pastels you work on a velvet-like paper. I was asked to come up with something different. "So I tried oils on velvet."

She also did nudes, a matter that involved her in public controversy when some were hung in the Polynesian restaurant of Vancouver's Waldorf Hotel. During our visit at her home she told me: "You should see the looks I get from my neighbors when I hang a nude in velvet on the clothes line to dry."

She said her greatest satisfaction comes from painting life-like portraits of ethnic types and gets particular delight from doing originals of Orientals and Hawaiians. She had just spent two weeks in Honolulu where she found models on the beaches and streets and in restaurants to pose for 25 paintings later displayed and sold in Victoria and Vancouver. She was about to fill a request from singer Frankie Laine to do his portrait before returning to Hawaii to prepare paintings for a show in California, where she had won several awards.

She sold Laughing Boy to me for $25. We stayed in touch. I did some writing for her use and when in New York helped her contact Time magazine about possible publication of her art. My files today still contain hand-written letters from Joy. In one, she told me she'd opened an art gallery in Honolulu's Hilton Hawaiian Village Hotel and described painting a portrait of actress Frances Nuyen of "South Pacific" fame. She also told me how she came to meet Stanley Kramer, the movie producer who commissioned her to do oil on velvet portraits of the 13 stars of his comedy "It's a Mad, Mad, Mad, Mad World."

The portraits were of Spencer Tracy, Jonathan Winters, Milton Berle, Sid Ceasar, Buddy Hackett, Ethel Merman, Mickey Rooney, Phil Silvers, Jimmy Durante, Edie Adams, Dorothy Provine, Dick Shawn and Terry Thomas.

Caros said "I got a phone call at home in my studio that Mr. Kramer would like to buy my painting of a girl with a candle, so I went down to the art shop." Kramer bought that one and two more, spotted a painting of a Hawaiian Boy which Caros described as "a little crying clown" and wanted to buy it as well.

It was owned by the manager of the Hawaiian Village Hotel who made a gift of it to Kramer. That's when Kramer commissioned Caros to do the clowns from his movie.

In a follow-up note, she described her preparation of works for a show in Welland, Ontario that led to a TV appearance in Toronto; wrote about a Las Vegas show and about the potential of being sent by Air France to Tahiti to do Tahitian portraits for use in brochures. An article dated March 21, 1963, and edited here for brevity, reported under a New York dateline:

> Vancouver artist Joy Caros, working in a field shunned by many of the purists, has reached another Plateau in her rapid rise to prominence as a painter working with oils on black velvet.
>
> New works by the 30-year-old housewife and mother of three, who during the last six years has developed a unique black velvet technique, will be shown in a Hollywood-style splash in New York City this fall. Canadians, however, will get first public look at the paintings scheduled for display here. Caros will show them in a collection of 35 of her works in Welland, Ont., starting April 25. From Ontario, the paintings will be taken to Las Vegas for a showing at the Sands.
>
> United artists said plans for New York include a television appearance and a theatre lobby display during the world premiere of the Kramer "Mad World" comedy.
>
> All of the above put Caros on her own mad, mad, whirl. To Hollywood, back to Vancouver, and back to Hollywood to complete the clowns. "Wow," she wrote.

Over the years, I followed Joy's career through on-line and other news reports, including one in The Georgia Straight by Charlie Smith, January 2010. Smith reported:

*Remember the Good Times*

A Vancouver artist's portraits of all of Israel's presidents and prime ministers will soon be on display in the corridors of power in Jerusalem. In a phone interview with the Straight, Joy Caros said she has completed paintings of 19 of the 20 people who've served as that country's president or prime minister, and she will soon finish a portrait of the last person on her list, Ariel Sharon.

"The paintings are on their way already," Caros said on January 4. "I think they arrive today." She plans to bring the portrait of Sharon with her when she visits the country in late May for an official unveiling.

Just over a decade ago, to commemorate Israel's 50th anniversary, she donated her collection of paintings of Israel's leaders to the Canadian Friends of the Hebrew University of Jerusalem. The CFHU's national director, Rami Kleinmann, told the Straight by phone from Ottawa that his organization is lending the portraits to the Israeli government for an unlimited time.

Caros, a Christian, said she decided to paint Israel's leaders in the 1990s because she appreciates how much various Jewish people have helped her career as an artist. In the 1960s, she worked with several Jewish directors in Hollywood, including Stanley Kramer, and painted portraits of all of the stars in Kramer's hit 1963 film It's a Mad, Mad, Mad, Mad World.

She pointed out that Israel, unlike Canada, doesn't commission artists to create portraits of its leaders. "It's a great thing to do for a country that hasn't been able to have that done," Caros said. "They supported me all my life."

NO DOUBT in my mind she's had a successful career over more than half a century and having a small role in all of that gives "Laughing Boy" a significant value in my memories.

## 14

# VOLUNTEERING BEGAN IN GLENAYRE

Volunteering in the community really started early in our time living in Glenayre, a neighborhood built in the 1950s and 60s as a Port Moody subdivision of about 500 single-family homes. We purchased a three-bedroom no-basement house at 482 Glencoe Drive, moved into it in December 1958, kept it when we moved to New York at the end of 1962 and eventually moved to a larger house at 902 Garrow Drive, just a few blocks from the Glencoe site. In July 2018, Glenayre celebrated its 60$^{th}$ anniversary.

When we moved to 482 Glencoe, the street came to an abrupt end half a block from our house. A school was built across the street from us. At about the same time, a portable building was put in place at the then end of Glencoe – to serve a United Church congregation. Out of curiosity, I attended a meeting there and wound up as Secretary to the Board. The building didn't succeed for long in its church mode, and as Secretary I was soon accepting resignations from Board members. A transition occurred and the portable did serve Glenayre residents for several years as a community hall and kindergarten site.

It was the base for many events, including an annual Easter

Egg Hunt where Jean and I and our daughters regularly attended. In 1960 our daughter, Kerry, went home with a giant chocolate bunny, won for being — at about two weeks old — the youngest participant. The family returned to this event several times over ensuing years with grandchildren Bryce, Keegan, Hallie and Zoey and, of course, their Parents, Ginny and Lance and Peggi and Phil.

The facility became the home of the Glenayre Community Association, which in 1993 brought residents together to raise funds and build a new community centre with space for a pre-school, events and meetings. Long before then I was president of the Association for one term at a time when it appeared to be dying. Those involved at the time kept it alive. And it continues as this is written.

The Centre became a party place for many residents, including those from Foress and Garrow Drives, who staged a friendly street golf competition, played several times at the Mission Golf Course, and always followed by cocktails, beer and wine and a fried chicken dinner from the Brownie's franchise of Glenayre residents Jack and Charleen Lynn.

The facility has special meaning for Jean and me – we rented it in 2001 and held a 50$^{th}$ wedding anniversary party there. And our family and I returned there on October 13$^{th}$, 2018, to celebrate Jean's life, which ended September 19, 2018 at Eagle Ridge Hospital.

The Port Moody Aquarians was another family and volunteer focal point for us. It is a summer swim club in which all three daughters took part in training and swim competitions from May through August. As parents, Jean and I were active on the pool deck, using stop watches as race timers, stroke judging and doing other such tasks. I undertook to publicize the competitions, writing reports after each one and delivering them to local newspapers in the Tri-Cities, New Westminster and Burnaby. The New West Columbian on one occasion published the entire story under my byline!

*Remember the Good Times*

Daughter Peggi took to the pools with considerable success, earned accreditation as a lifeguard, made life-long friendships with teammates and competitors from other communities, and eventually earned a swim scholarship that helped pay her way through Simon Fraser University where she earned a BA, majoring in Communication.

All of that experience served her well over the years as she added a year-long Asian studies course at Capilano College that included an overseas job posting. In Peggi's case, the job entailed research and writing for periodicals. She was based in Bangkok, Thailand and her work took her to several other locations, including Burma.

She combined that educational background with her public relations and other writing experience and parlayed them into a public relations assignment with Northern Telecom in Hong Kong. Jean visited Peggi there, on another of her solo travel adventures, taking a flight from Vancouver with just a small carry-on bag as a courier delivering important checked luggage for her sponsor who paid the air fare. She never forgot the excitement and pleasure of that trip and her exploration of Hong Kong under Peggi's guidance.

Not long after her Mother's visit Peggi moved from Hong Kong to Vietnam where she lived in Ho Chi Minh City (formerly Saigon) – and opened the J. Walter Thompson advertising agency, then helped to build it into the largest ad agency in the country. Jean and I were both able to visit her over a Christmas-New Year trip from December 20, 1995 to January 7, 1996, starting with Air Canada's inaugural flight from Vancouver to Hong Kong.

We travelled with Peggi as our host and benefactor to Bangkok, then to the Phuket's Banyan Tree

*Jean, Peggi and Jean's ride in Hanoi*

resort on the Andaman Sea and to Ho Chi Minh City and Hanoi in Vietnam.

When Peggi returned to British Columbia following the British hand-over of Hong Kong on January 1, 1997, she brought with her an electrical engineer she'd met in Vietnam – Phil Jones, P. Eng. with a Master's degree in Electrical Engineering earned at Georgia Tech. They were married on August 9, 1997, atop Saturna Island, travelled much of British Columbia in a Volkswagen van as their honeymoon trip and soon began a family. Hallie Nissa was born July 15, 1998 and Zoey Shea arrived August 26, 2000. Both Hallie and Zoey were Aquarian team members for a time, Hallie focusing on diving and winning trophies, Zoey honing skills to lifeguard as her Mother had done.

*Peggi and Phil wedding*

Peggi later returned to university to expand her skills, earning a Master's in Journalism from the University of British Columbia.

## 15

# A GREAT FAMILY NEIGHBORHOOD

GOOD GOLF AND PERSONAL TIMES AND FUND-RAISING

Glenayre was a great place to live and raise our family. We met our neighbors, participated with them in community events and civic politics, got involved with golf, including membership at the Pitt Meadows Golf Club and became part of a group of 16 who partied together at Grey Cup, New Year's Eve and Super Bowl dates for dozens of years.

In the earliest years of our lives in this subdivision, we met, dined and socialized with Lyall and Phyllis Hawkins, Jim and Greta Smith and Bob and Rosetta Smith (not related) all of them among the first to settle in Glenayre.

Lyall and Phyllis were members of Pitt Meadows Golf Club and convinced us to join there, too. We saved up $50 to pay the entry fee and committed to $10 a month to cover two $100 debentures. As our daughters grew older and demanded more attention, Jean gave up her membership and pretty much abandoned golf except for some rounds played with neighbors on shorter, executive or par-three courses as a prelude to partying.

I continued as a member through 2018 and recall many fun rounds with Lyall, Jock Anderson and his wife Mary, Terry Nelford (PGA pro Jim Nelford's father), Frank Smith and wife

JIM PEACOCK

Vera, brothers Hal and Dennis McLennan, Allan Sinclair, and through them, long-time partner Richard Stewart who in 2018 continued to best me when he was turning 93. Dennis, Richard and I also played with Mark Franklin for a time after Allan moved to Granisle in the Courtenay-Comox area of Vancouver Island.

Dennis, Allan, Dick and I did road trips together for three or four years, loading our gear into an SUV, driving to Kamloops, Salmon Arm and Kelowna to golf at several courses – on the way to Kamloops, in the Kamloops area, in the Salmon Arm area and at Kelowna, sometimes with a stop at Chilliwack on the way home. We also did a couple of tours of Vancouver Island after Allan's move.

*Golf road trip companions, l to r, Allan Sinclair, Dick Stewart, Dennis McLennan*

I also played in and helped organize and promote many charitable golf events, some supporting the Variety club and some, including one I started on Vancouver Island, in support of Ronald McDonald House and Ronald McDonald Children's Charities.

On one occasion, an event supporting the Variety Club, I was teamed up with Barbara Stewart whose husband Bob was then the Chief of Police in Vancouver. Over time, both served terms as

*Remember the Good Times*

Chief Barker (president) of Tent 47. On this golf outing I was able to claim that "I played a round with the police chief's wife and got away with it."

The Arbutus Ridge Golf Club near Duncan on Vancouver Island was a client of Terry McDowell, advertising manager at MacMillan Bloedel when I worked there and at this point resident in the MacFarlane Peacock agency's offices. In 1992, Terry brought the golf course to the table with the goal being to publicize this then new layout. I brought the McDonald's charity causes and the McDonald's franchisees of the Island along and drew on past friendships with several Victoria media personalities to promote the event.

I hired help — Rita Cruerer. I had met her through the Variety Club and my participation in another RMCC golf tournament at the UBC Golf Course. She eventually became an associate of Peacock Public Relations and later its Vice-President, working with me on several accounts, including the Vancouver Community Centre Association Presidents in campaigns to encourage voter support for capital investment in community centre renewal. By my recollection, in the first year of the Vancouver Island Ronald House golf tournament, we turned over $6,000 to the McDonald's charities.

As this tournament grew, it attracted more celebrities, among them the late LPGA professional Dawn Coe Jones, who grew up in the Cowichan Valley area where Arbutus Ridge Golf Club is located. At one of the tournaments, Dawn arrived just as I was about to use a power golf cart to move my golf clubs from my car to the club's tee-off area, so I gave her a ride to the clubhouse. Several years later, when she was among the TV commentators covering the 2012 Canadian Women's Open at the Vancouver Golf Club in Coquitlam where I worked as a volunteer we remembered the Arbutus Ridge ride during a conversation outside the press tent. That was the year Lydia Ko of New Zealand, at 15 still an amateur, won the tournament.

## 16

## GLENAYRE YEARS OF FUN CELEBRATIONS

Back in Glenayre, following several New Year's celebrations in the gym of the elementary school, where most of the residents showed up, our party group evolved to include eight couples: Jean and me, Bruce and Eunice Nicoll, Jack and June Elliott, David and Diana Finlay, Don and Lynne Monk, Dan and Carolyn McArdle, Norm and Noreen Sherling and Harold and Bonnie Mulzet.

Our first year with them all marked the start of 1982 and brought us together at the home of Bruce and Eunice Nicoll who lived across Clarke Street in a home near Porter in Coquitlam. Bruce was head of Canada Safeway in the region and the Nicolls were good friends of Don and Lynne Monk. Don was also with Safeway in a labour relations post.

The following years rotated from home to home – the McArdles, the Elliotts, the Finlays, and after a year in Calgary the Nicolls returned to a new home in Coquitlam and again hosted the group. We were hosts for the first time to bring in the 1987 New Year. On occasion, the group chose a neutral location, as happened when we went to the Sundance Ranch near Ashcroft to bring in 1990; to the Semiahmoo Resort Hotel in Washington state

JIM PEACOCK

to end 1991; to Harrison Hot Springs resort for 1992 and to a waterfront hotel at Cowichan Bay on Vancouver Island, where the Sherlings arrived aboard their own boat.

We began the new millennium – 2000 — at our house, went to the New Year's eve party at Pitt Meadows Golf Club to launch 2002 and two years later went to a production of 42$^{nd}$ Street at the then Ford Theatre in Vancouver.

*Noreen, Diana, June, Carolyn and Jean, New Year's at Pitt Meadows*

*Danny, Jack, David, Norman, NY's at Pitt Meadows*

*Remember the Good Times*

All of the above dates are courtesy of Noreen Sherling, who put in a great deal of time and effort coordinating arrangements for each of the New Year's Eve events and kept meticulous records that even noted our daughter Virginia and husband Lance attended the 42$^{nd}$ Street evening in place of the Elliotts who were ill.

No one recorded all of the details for the Grey Cup and Super Bowl parties, but they went on annually during the same stretch. We didn't do the New Year's Eve stint to mark the beginning of 2006, but we capped off that party string with a 10-day cruise that began January 9 in San Francisco aboard the Dawn Princess, making stops at Catalina Island, Peurto Vallarta, Mazatlan, Cabo San Lucas and San Diego before returning to San Francisco.

*A post-New Year's cruise from San Francisco saw a dozen of our Glenayre Gang sailing under the Golden Gate bridge*

Jean and I were able to include a visit with Peggy and Stuart Matheson enroute, which added to the fun. By then, Jack and June Elliott were spending winter months in Arizona and flew over from there to join the rest of us on the cruise.

JIM PEACOCK

*Stuart and Peggy Matheson*

When we returned to the West Coast from New York in 1964 our children were reaching school age. They all attended Glenayre Elementary, walking with their friends a couple of blocks from home to school and back, coming home for lunches, playing in the streets where they rode their tricycles and learned to ride bicycles. Other families did the same thing in complete safety with none of the fears that entered much of our society at later times.

Jean strolled the neighborhood, too, and, with a walking stick for her protection against any wildlife she might encounter, walked the trails on the adjacent Burnaby Mountain. For more than a dozen years, she had as her companion a somewhat overgrown but registered miniature Schnauzer nick-named Stach, for his mustachioed face.

After more than a dozen years with Jean – who took Stach to a doggie training course and later claimed that Stach passed but Jean failed – Stach went to doggie heaven. By that time, we had somewhere acquired a key ring with a pewter representation of a Schnauzer that looked much like Stach. Jean cherished the key ring as a reminder of so many good times with her pooch, Then Stach the key ring disappeared, too. Search as we might, we could not find it.

In the spring of 2003 we began planning another excursion and we discovered it had a link to Glenayre memories. It came in

*Remember the Good Times*

March and April, 2003. The Balcom family – Ginny, Lance, Bryce and Keegan had decided to devote a year to world travel. (Virginia met Lance Balcom while both were studying Mechanical Engineering at the University of British Columbia and they were married aboard the paddlewheeler cruise boat Constitution in Vancouver Harbour on December 30, 1983. Their family tour included a visit to Spain. Peggi was in Vietnam with J. Walter Thompson advertising and a colleague from London offered use of a waterfront condo he owned on the Mediterranean coast, at Soto Grande.

Jean and I booked flights with Air Canada and flew with AC's partner, Lufthansa, from Vancouver to Frankfurt on the way to meet the Balcoms in Soto Grande. We were boarding our aircraft in Vancouver when suddenly on Jean's seat there appeared a Stach key ring – the German pooch on a German airliner decided to come out of hiding. Apparently, this Stach had hidden away in the lining of a raincoat and when Jean took off the coat to place it in the overhead bin, Stach the keyring escaped from its hiding place.

That all occurred in the year before we sold our Glenayre house and moved to NewPort Village, into a 21$^{st}$ floor sub-penthouse condo where we lived together for more than 13 years. Stach the keyring held fob and keys to that suite until the condo was sold in 2019.

We met the Balcoms in Soto Grande. Jean and I stayed in a three-level, two-bedroom suite overlooking a yacht basin and beach from which Gibraltar was in clear view, often behind high flying kiteboarders riding the wind above the sea. From that base, we visited Gibraltar; Tangiers in Morocco where we all tried riding camels; and Alhambra, a palace and fortress complex in Granada, Andalusa, Spain.

Originally built in AD 889 on the remains of Roman fortifications, Alhambra is a major tourist attraction with carefully tended gardens and beautiful vistas. Grandson Bryce wowed many visitors in each of these locales by spinning along the cobblestone pathways on the rollers in the heels of his running shoes.

Among our adventures were shopping trips to supermarkets in nearby cities. Language challenges made some of the shopping outcomes near disastrous, among them purchase of a roasting chicken still with all of its innards intact. Jean, as usual, found a way to deal with it! We also discovered on some dining outings that drinking wine was less costly than drinking Coca Cola or other soft drinks.

On our travel home, Jean and I spent a day touring Frankfurt, a somewhat uneventful time where the most memorable thing was the size and scope of the airport.

## 17

# A SAFARI, LITERALLY AND FIGURATIVELY

FUND RAISING FOR LIBRARY AND CITY HALL

My Glenayre and Aquarian volunteer activities brought some attention in Port Moody. The Port Moody Foundation was established under the leadership of Ted Rathonyi-Reusz, City of Port Moody Parks & Recreation Director, and Councillor Ann Hulbert. Its formation was announced November 19, 1989. Councillor Hulbert's husband Peter was a news photographer with The Province. I knew them both from journalism days.

The initial meeting of the founding Directors took place April 11, 1989. The directors were Ann Hulbert, Jo-Anne Parneta, Jim Peacock, Ted Slinger and Donna Sweeney. I became the first elected president, a post I filled for six years. In that role, I became heavily involved in some major community events in Port Moody and in a sister community, in Africa — Kariba, Zimbabwe.

Whether it was my involvement with the Foundation or the volunteer work I did to promote an annual Port Moody Festival of the Arts I am not sure. Probably both. In any event, in the spring of 1992, I got a phone call from the city's mayor, David Driscoll. He had a some-times wry sense of humour and when he asked me if I'd like to join him on a safari, I thought he had some city location in mind for some purpose, not immediately defined. At the time, I was not a particular fan and, in fact I had campaigned on behalf of his opponent in the civic election that put him in office.

As it turned out, he was extending an invitation to me to join him and then City Administrator Les Harrington on a 10-day trip to the African country of Zimbabwe for an official exchange between our city and the community of Kariba. The exchange was part of the Federation of Canadian Municipalities (FCM) Africa 2000 program that established a link between the Town of Kariba and the City of Port Moody. The program began with our visit in May 1992. Two exploratory technical exchanges followed in the fall of 1992 and the spring of 1993.

A joint community project included fund-raising in Port Moody to support construction of the Nyamhunga playing field, including a base perimeter game-protection wall, changing rooms, toilet facilities and field-levelling to enable safe use. I learned soon enough that it was not just a 10-day commitment to travel. By accepting the invitation, I was agreeing to raise funds on my return to Port Moody to provide Kariba with the improved recreational facilities described above, facilities chosen by the Kariba Council and especially focused on the town's youth.

ON APRIL 30, 1992, I flew to London, where a day later I met up with Mayor Driscoll and City Manager Harrington. We flew from London to Harare, where we were invited by our hosts to a round of golf on a local course whose members were mostly from the Harare police force. We saw some of the luxury in which then President Robert Mugabe thrived and privately heard some of the stories of Mugabe's destructive handling of the transition from British to African rule as Rhodesia became Zimbabwe.

Enroute to Kariba, we also spent a night literally on safari in Hwange National Park, Zimbabwe's largest natural reserve, riding among lions, rhinos, elephants, monkeys and other wildlife. We then stayed overnight at Victoria Falls on the Zambezi River and had time to tour the Elephant Hills Golf Club with holes named Kudu Run, Buffalo Wallow, Impala Bend, Hippo Marsh, Warthog's Walk and where it was normal to see some of these animals alongside the fairways. The Zambezi is the fourth largest river in Africa, forms the border between Zimbabwe and Zambia and is the reason for Kariba's existence.

Victoria Falls is one of the great attractions in Africa; Scottish missionary-explorer David Livingstone named it after Queen Victoria following his 1855 discovery of what some describe as the largest fall in the world. The town of Kariba was developed in the 1950s to house workers building the Kariba power dam about 200 kilometres downstream from Victoria Falls on the Zambezi River. Behind the dam is Lake Kariba, one of the world's largest man-made lakes. The hydro-electric installation provides power to both Zimbabwe and Zambia.

Port Moody and Kariba were of about the same size with populations at the time in the range of 25,000. Elephants and Rhinos were in evidence most everywhere we went in Kariba, whose council had chosen the community project to be funded by Port Moody donors. Its perimeter wall was considered a necessity to restrict elephants from destroying the soccer field. We saw rhinos wallowing in sewage lagoons but they didn't seem to be considered a threat to the soccer pitch.

Among local council members we met was one young man who conducted training sessions for youth wanting to be tourist guides. But the community did not have a vehicle to transport tourists on the many roads criss-crossing the beautiful landscape or for use in the training. I drew on my Variety Club background to help them resolve that problem, arranging an application to Variety International for a $10,000 (U.S.) grant to purchase a small truck that Kariba's Council had converted to a 12-passenger bus, used for both training guides and transporting visitors.

After returning May 9, 1992 to Port Moody, I organized a

fund-raising program, focused on buying $25 bricks for the Elephant Wall, and with great help from the Coquitlam NOW and Tri-City News community newspapers, eventually made it possible for Port Moody to turn over the pledged funds, as well as the matching grant from CIDA (Canadian International Development Agency) which brought Kariba $30,000 toward the playing field project.

The NOW newspaper was involved at the time in an exchange program with Zimbabwe media and that took reporter Hazel Postma from the Tri-Cities to Kariba. The February 7, 1993 edition carried her by-lined article with a photo of the playing field area. "There are no recreation facilities," she wrote, "which is the reason a group of Port Moody residents has launched a campaign to raise $12,000 towards the development of a soccer field complete with change room and toilet facilities." I learned later that Kariba's council found that the planned wall wouldn't keep the elephants off the soccer pitch after all so they put the funds to other youth recreation purposes.

On my wall I have a numbered print of a drawing of the Port Moody C.P.R. Station by Danna Pe Akne that carries an engraved plaque reading:

### JIM PEACOCK
*With thanks from the people of Port Moody and Kariba*

In 1994, when the city was developing a new civic centre, including City Hall and Public Library at Inlet Centre, the Port Moody Foundation undertook to raise $375,000 for enhancement of these facilities. We launched the Legacy Capital Campaign in August. The Board of the Foundation then was Jim Peacock, President; Jo-Anne Parneta, Vice-President; Clare Hill, Treasurer; Wilda Booth, Secretary; Bob Gray, Chris Green, Peter Hulbert and Susan Staschuck, Directors. The Honorary Patrons were R.S. Bremner, then President and CEO, BCTV ; David Driscoll, former Mayor of Port Moody; Opera Diva and Port Moody resident

*Remember the Good Times*

Judith Forst; swim champion Kathy Glen; William Harris, General Manager, Pacific Coast Terminals; and ice-skater Tracy Wilson.

In the end, the campaign fell short of its goal but funding was generated to cover several elements of lasting benefit to the community. Royal Bank Charitable Foundation, through its local branch manager, funded an infra-red Listening Assist System for the City Council Chamber-cum-Inlet Theatre to enhance listening for those with hearing impairments. ParkLane Homes funded a Presentation Room, Aragon Development Corporation a Children's Story Telling Room, Petro Canada a Study Alcove, and Ronald McDonald's Children's Charities multi-level workstations to serve special needs children in the new public Library that was largely funded separately by Bosa Developments. Imperial Oil's Ioco Refinery supported seats in the theatre and Canadian Pacific Charitable Foundation funded the theatre's refreshment centre.

More than 50 individuals, a half dozen community organizations, including the local branch of the Royal Canadian Legion, several large and small businesses active in Port Moody made $200 per seat contributions to support theatre seat installation and, while the Stage 43 theatre group reneged on a $16,200 pledge toward that end, the Inlet Theatre wound up with seating capacity of 200. Donors were acknowledged in plaques attached to seats in the theatre and on a donor wall in the lobby of City Hall. That wall carries these names:

**Platinum Donors**
Imperial Oil Limited Ioco Refinery
Royal Bank of Canada

**Gold Donors**
Canadian Pacific Charitable Foundation

JIM PEACOCK

**Silver Donors**
Jack and Ginger Cewe
John L. Northey
Donna Otto & Rev. David Spence
Pacific Coast Terminals Co. Ltd.
Peacock Public Relations

MY LAST YEAR as Foundation President was 1994-95. Jo-Anne Parneta succeeded me as president. Rick Nelson served on the board for a time and in 2000 succeeded Jo-Anne. Dan Brown succeeded Rick in the presidency, was followed by Rev. David Spence and, in 2002, by Robert Simons. Rick was President during the Old Mill Boathouse fund-raising campaign, in which I contributed to communications activities to help Gordon Clay, then President of the Old Mill Boathouse, in his long-standing quest to get the community and the City behind building the $1.2 million boathouse that was opened in 2002. The building provides rowers, sailors and paddlers with club meeting rooms, washrooms, showers and storage space for non-power boats. Its large meeting space, called the Great Room, also serves many other community groups as a place to stage events.

## 18

# NEW YORK EXCITEMENT AND ENTERTAINMENT

New York had provided some excitement for Jean and me in earlier visits, including dinner in 1954 with Don and Virginia Gilbert, Don then the New York CP Bureau Chief. The Gilberts lived in the NYC suburb of White Plains. A press pass from Don enabled my attendance at the aforementioned World Series baseball game between the Giants and the Indians. We got to know the Gilberts in Edmonton during my first time working in that CP bureau and were so fond of Don's wife that we chose her name for our first-born. Unfortunately, Don died way too soon – in 1959 – three years before I was assigned to New York.

Our 1963 arrival in New York with three young children came in the midst of a newspaper strike that created challenges in finding a place to live. No want-ads listing rentals, except in smaller community papers. We settled, for a while, in an upstairs suite owned by a young couple whose demands made our lives so miserable we soon moved on to a small house across from an elementary school in Bergenfield, New Jersey.

The commuting time for me, to Rockefeller Centre in Manhattan, where CP shared office space with The Associated Press and

NBC, was nearly two hours each way, travelling by bus and subway. That left responsibility for the kids largely on Jean's shoulders and precious little time for me to spend with the family.

Nonetheless, there were some pleasant memories established during our New York sojourn, among them our first family visit to a McDonald's restaurant long before we had any inkling how big a role that organization would have later in our lives. It was a time when Mickey Mantle and Roger Maris were New York Yankee stars. At the McDonald's, we couldn't help notice two very attractive young women with their children enjoying burgers and fries. We learned later they were Mrs. Mantle and Mrs. Maris.

My CP assignment in New York was focused on editing news copy from AP for redistribution to Canada's news media through the CP teletype network. But opportunities for research, interviews and reporting – especially where there was a Canadian aspect to the story – were encouraged. Mantle and Maris were among those I was privileged to meet in interviews at Yankee Stadium during batting practise one day. I talked with Casey Stengel at the old Polo Grounds and reported on his quotes about a couple of young Canadian players making the scene at the time.

I visited the Manhattan apartment of Ed Sullivan to talk with him about the significance of Wayne and Shuster and other Canadian performers, including Toronto-born ballerina Melissa Hayden, who were appearing on the TV variety show he so successfully hosted for years. An interview with Hayden, who became a principal dancer with the New York City Ballet, in her apartment overlooking Central Park, occurred when her book "Melissa Hayden, Offstage and On" was published while we were in New York.

One of my first encounters with an activist Canadian aboriginal came in March 1963 when Kahn-Tineta Horn, a 22-year-old Mohawk who grew up on the Caughnawaga Reservation near Montreal, was educated in Montreal, New York and Paris visited

*Remember the Good Times*

New York to appear at a toy display that included Princess Kanata dolls she had designed in her own likeness for a Toronto toy company. She also designed the clothing for the doll.

She earned a living then as a model and a writer but devoted much of her time to improving the lot of her people, among other things serving as a director with the National Indian Council of Canada, which took her to settlements across the country. The Council honored her in 1963 by naming her the first Princess Canada of Canadian Indians, a word still in wide use at that time. The Weekend magazine supplement published in Montreal featured her as a cover girl about 18 months before the New York toy show, where I talked with her and reported:

> "The question brought Kahn-Tineta Horn's sparkling brown eyes up from the yogurt-and-honey lunch she was having at a plush mid-Manhattan hotel. She looked straight up at the questioner and replied: 'For quite a few years you know, I've been an Indian.' She had been asked what prompted her to apply so much of her time and energies to efforts to bring improvement to the circumstances of the Canadian Indian. Her answer seemed startling at first, but on examination it explained simply and succinctly the motivation behind this young woman's enthusiasm for the activities she pursued."

The summer of 1963 brought another prominent Canadian to New York. Golfer Stan Leonard. He talked to me during a practise round at the Westchester Country Club for the $100,000 Thunderbird Open. My report from Harrison, N.Y. started: "Pro (for professor) Stan Leonard paused between shots to wax enthusiastic about going to college. Not just any college – but a golf college for youngsters who have aspirations and promise in golf." The rest of the article focused on Leonard's plans to support this "college" plan at the Chillwack, B.C. Golf Club to provide professional instruction in physical education and golf to as many as 150 players aged 12 to 20 years.

Colleen Dewhurst, an actress born in Montreal, the daughter of one-time Ottawa Rough Rider football player Fred Dewhurst, was playing Cleopatra in the New York Shakespeare Festival's Central Park presentation of "Anthony and Cleopatra" when I asked her why she worked six nights a week for three weeks for $500 when she could command much more elsewhere. "There's something about doing Shakespeare here that is completely different from anywhere else," she said. "Here'" was the Delecorte Theatre in Central Park, its stage backdrop containing a lake, rock outcroppings and nature's greenery. It is a delightful outdoor theatre where occasionally an aircraft flying over drowns out a syllable or two. Miss Dewhurst gestured toward the broad expanse of the wide-open stage and said: "It gives you a great sense of freedom. You can really let go."

The audience also creates a special sensation for the performers. Every night 2,300 people fill every seat, the price of a ticket being only the time spent standing in line to get it. Admission is free – the cost of the production being paid by theatre patrons and the City of New York. Miss Dewhurst, married to actor George Scott, added: "It's amazing to see 2,300 people sitting out there every night."

Another Montreal-born actress was making headlines then, not just for her career success but for her involvement in the civil rights movement in the Southern U.S. Over lunch at Sardi's, I met with Madeleine Sherwood who starred as the Reverend Mother Placido to Sally Field's Sister Bertille in TV's The Flying Nun, 1967 – 1970. Our discussion focused on work she had done with Martin Luther King Jr. and on her recent protest visit to Selma, Alabama. She went south to join CORE (Congress on Racial Equality) and during a Freedom Walk she was arrested, jailed and sentenced to six months hard labor, for endangering the Customs and Mores of the People of Alabama. She was freed on $1,000 bail, pending further hearings.

I researched and wrote a series of articles related to racial unrest in the northern U.S. where, unlike the Southern states, laws had changed in attempts to create equality but in practice subtle discrimination continued. Those were tense times in the U.S. and the tension was palpable when, as part of the research for the civil rights articles, I paid a visit to the offices of the NAACP (National Association for the Advancement of Colored People) in Harlem. Walking those streets was, plain and simple, scary. Enlightening as to how others in a minority situation may feel, and scary.

While I was doing these things, Jean was taking care of Ginny, Kerry and Peggi; getting to know our neighbors, especially Dorothy Hearn, her son Steve and daughter Susan who lived in a house similar to our rental and right next door. Fortunately, Jean got to share in some of the perks. CP received tickets to second night performances of new Broadway productions. These were distributed among CP staff members. Jean and I were able to attend the second night of Hello Dolly, starring Carol Channing, in the St. James Theatre, a marvellous and memorable experience made affordable for us by those tickets.

We got to see other Broadway hits, including "A Funny Thing Happened on the way to the Forum", starring Zero Mostell, and watched in awe as the Rockettes danced in unison across the stage at Radio City music Hall. There were visits to such interesting locales as the united Nations Building, the Museum of Modern Art, the Waldorf Hotel, even Coney Island and some fun lunches beside the ice rink in Rockefeller Center.

I reported on some events at the United Nations, including a news conference with the Hon. Paul Martin, then External Affairs Minister in the Lester Pearson government in Ottawa. I made copious notes during some 30 minutes, but when I read those notes I found Martin had really said nothing worth reporting that day, no matter how important it all sounded at the time.

## 19

# MY BIGGEST NEWS ASSIGNMENT

In November 1963, I spent two weeks, working about 12 hours a day, covering a convention of the U.S. labour organizations, AFL/CIO, to report on issues of great interest at the time to media in Montreal where controversy swirled around the Seafarers International Union. The issues had to do with SIU leadership in Canada, where the Federal government had placed the union under trusteeship.

Something that is still with me is the fact that President John F. Kennedy was to address the AFL/CIO (American Federation of Labor/Congress of Industrial Organizations) convention on Friday, November 15, 1963 – and the CP Chief of Bureau decided to rely on The AP to provide CP's coverage of that speech. I was ready for a rest but disappointed that I wouldn't see The President up close and personally.

That sense of disappointment took a huge leap a week later. I was in charge of our kids, lolling in our house and listening to jazz, undoubtedly including some by Lena Horne, a favorite of mine who, as described in more detail elsewhere, I was privileged to spend 30 minutes with at a rehearsal interview when she played The Cave night club in Vancouver in July 1962. Jean was at a neighborhood salon having her hair done in preparation for an evening party with other Canadian media posted in New York. The occasion was to mark the transfer back to Canada of a CBC news correspondent.

> Our phone rang and the female voice said: "I guess the party is off." I said: "Oh. Why?" Her response: "Kennedy's been shot."

I hung up the phone, turned on the TV and caught up with the biggest news I would encounter in my career. A few minutes later, my phone rang again. It was the CP Bureau Chief. He told me CP's Washington, D.C. correspondent, Harold Morrison was out of town on an assignment and was being sent to Dallas, where President Kennedy was shot while with riding his wife in the back of an open convertible carrying them on a parade through the city. The rest of that day is history that doesn't need repeating here.

Jean came home from the salon, where everything had stopped when the news broke. I got a cab to the Newark Airport and flew to Washington, checking in with the media relations people at The White House soon after arriving. I watched on a TV placed outdoors between the driveway and the White House as cameras in Dallas caught Jack Ruby shooting Lee Harvey Oswald, the accused killer of President Kennedy.

I remember going to the Pentagon location where world leaders gathered as they arrived. They walked along a roped off sidewalk, acknowledging people lined on either side. Among them was President Charles de Gaulle of France, who I recall sought out attractive women and greeted them with a kiss on the hand, demonstrating to me, at least, a typical French romanticism.

*Remember the Good Times*

*Montreal Star photo of Prime Minister Pearson, speaking with media – Jim Peacock, not identified in the caption.*

Canada's Prime Minister Lester Pearson was among those gathering there and I was among the news media covering his news conference. Later, I received a copy of the second front page of the November 25, 1963 Montreal Star, filled with photos of leaders who came to Washington for the funeral. One of The Star's photos was a close-up of Pearson with a front view of a reporter beside him with this caption: "Prime Minister Lester Pearson talks to reporters on his arrival in Washington last night to attend funeral services for President John F. Kennedy." The reporter in the picture was me.

I stood outside the White House on the Sunday of the funeral to get a close-up view of the procession – and when Life magazine published its John F. Kennedy Memorial Edition, its back cover displayed a photo of his widow, Jacqueline, daughter Caroline and son John Jr. Part of the photo shows a group standing beside the driveway and, if you know who you're looking for, you'll find me there. A copy of that 50-cent purchase is among my treasured keepsakes.

## 20

# MOVING BACK TO THE WEST COAST

One of my last pieces from New York in April 1964 appeared under the heading 100 Million expected to visit New York Fair and read:

"The official countdown clock ticks and clicks amid the hustle and bustle of feverish construction activity in Flushing Meadows these last hectic days before the opening of the billion-dollar New York World's Fair. The electronic clock in the fair's administration building will hit zero hour at 9 a.m. EST Wednesday, April 22, and the gates will be opened to the public, Before the gates are shut for the last time Oct. 17, 1965 after two six-month runs interrupted by a winter closing, as many as 100,000,000 people are expected to crowd the 646-acre showplace to see the wonders of past, present and future from many lands."

Jean and I were talking then about how long our meagre savings would last if we stayed in the New York area. In Vancouver, meanwhile, a promoter named William Val Warren was making plans to start a new daily newspaper. He hired William Forst as the editorial director; I knew Bill Forst from early days

JIM PEACOCK

with CP in Vancouver when Bill was Managing Editor of The Province. CP's offices were in The Province building.

To make a long story short, I contacted Bill, worked out a deal to join The Times and have The Times cover part of our cost to move back to Vancouver, where we still owned the first house we purchased in the Glenayre subdivision of Port Moody.

We made the long drive from our Bergenfield, New Jersey rental to Calgary in the same vehicle that took us to New York. We arrived in New York in a new maroon 1962 Ford station wagon, picked up at the Oakville, Ontario factory where it was made; drove it during our stay there as residents of Bergenfield and drove it back to Calgary and then to Vancouver, going through Chicago on the way.

I was to return to Chicago a couple of times to attend McDonald's public relations conferences and during one of those, I had my first of several opportunities to see a Circ du Soleil performance in a tent theatre. Jean and I attended a couple more of those in Vancouver; Jean also viewed the special water show of Circ in Las Vegas during an all-girls visit to celebrate Keegan's coming-of-age 21$^{st}$ birthday, and all of our grandchildren became Circ fans. Hallie and Zoey enrolled in a program called Circ Kids and learned a lot of circus tricks. Hallie still surprises her Queen's classmates on occasion, riding a unicycle on campus.

The Ford Fairlane was one of many automobiles we drove over the years, among them a used Chrysler sedan that we drove from Toronto to Calgary on one summer vacation, being entertained along the way by a friend and violinist named Betty Grabiedoff who later became a member of Calgary's symphony orchestra.

Among the vehicles I recall were two red Mustang convertibles, a pale blue two-seat convertible sports Midget, a 1957 Chevrolet, an eight-cylinder gas guzzler Chev Sedan with an eight-track tape player that Jean drove from Vancouver to Calgary and to Fort St. John. We eventually sold the Chevy to a music group who used its huge trunk to carry their instruments.

*Remember the Good Times*

We had a Hillman, a Morris Minor and a couple of others, one of them a red Ford Bronco, before our final series that included a red GMC Envoy and what I've called my 2010 Olympics "silver medal" – a silver Chev Equinox purchased for me by Kerry from the fleet used in the 2010 Winter Games in Vancouver and still with fewer than 50,000 kilometres recorded as we entered 2019.

ON OUR RETURN TO VANCOUVER, Jean and our three daughters spent time with Grandma Lottie Hembree in Calgary while I went on to the West Coast, staying with Jean's brother Dave, his wife Edith and their children Karen and Dick at a Burnaby residence just a few minutes from The Times location at Broadway and Rupert in Vancouver.

The editorial staff of The Times, which included Doug Collins, Jack Webster, Jim Taylor – all of them well established in the Vancouver news market as reporters and/or columnists — was being assembled and working toward a Sept. 5, 1964 first edition.

On that date, The Times began its competition to the morning tabloid, The Province, and the then afternoon broadsheet, The Sun, with an exclusive report: "LBJ asks Pearson to meet him here" the headline above a story by Dillon O'Leary, the Times Ottawa correspondent, who wrote: "President Johnson has invited Prime Minister Pearson to meet him in Vancouver on Sept. 16. The two would then drive to Seattle for a day of celebrations marking the exchange of ratification papers on the Columbia River treaty."

My first byline in The Times was related: On Page 2, under the heading: "Columbia cheque early" I wrote: "The U.S. will pay B.C. two weeks early for Columbia River power benefits and the decision means money saved for both B.C. and the U.S. utilities group putting up the cash. B.C. will get an added benefit in a two-week head-start on major construction on the multi-million-dollar project. Premier W.A.C. Bennett announced Friday that a cheque for $275 million (Canadian) will be turned over to B.C.

Sept. 16—a full 15 days ahead of the Oct. 1 deadline set in the Columbia treaty."

In the Nov. 19, 1964 edition, the front-page headline read: Two to challenge Dief? My story started; "Reports prevalent in B.C. today indicate two contenders for the leadership of the Conservative party will declare themselves this weekend. They are Premier Robert Stanfield of Nova Scotia and E. Davie Fulton, former federal Justice Minister and currently B.C. Conservative leader." (Stanfield was the eventual choice to succeed Diefenbaker who was forced out of the Party Leadership in 1967.)

The Times survived only a few months and by the time it ceased publication I was employed by the Vancouver Sun as assistant business editor. While at the Times, I was recruited by reporter Simma Holt who authored a book "Terror in the Name of God" about the Doukhobor sect in the Kootenay area of southern British Columbia. I was hired by Erwin Swanguard, The Sun's Managing Editor. I had become acquainted with both during my work with CP in Vancouver.

## 21

# ONION SOUP AND ANOTHER CAREER MOVE

RECONNECTION WITH THE HEMBREE KIDS

Six months later, my career took another turn over an "onion soup" served in a chilled, stemmed glass.

Don Tyreman was a Vice-President of O'Brien Advertising Ltd., an agency owned and operated by Michael J. O'Brien, better known as Mickey. Don invited me to lunch in the dining room of the Ritz Hotel on West Georgia, next door to the Burrard Building at the corner of Georgia and Burrard Streets directly across Burrard from the Hotel Vancouver.

As a frequent patron of the Ritz dining room, Don was known to the serving staff and the one who took his order that day, asked "What will you have today?" Don replied: "Oh, the usual onion soup." I said: "That sounds good to me. I'll have the same."

Then I realized Don had ordered a vodka martini, distinguished from a gin martini by the tiny pickled onion in the glass rather than the typical gin martini olive. We both enjoyed the tipsy; Don offered an opportunity to join O'Brien Consultants Ltd. in a public and media relations role, with my first client to be the British Columbia Telephone Company. I met Mickey O'Brien and other members of his agency and signed on.

B.C. Telephone Company later adopted the name BC Tel and

JIM PEACOCK

still later after a merger it became TELUS. For the purposes, here, I will refer to the company as BC Tel.

On June 28, 1965 I joined O'Brien Consultants. That was the beginning of a career in agency and corporate public relations that continued until December 2004 when Peacock Public Relations Ltd. was formally dissolved.

I spent seven years with O'Brien Consultants, and became its president and CEO. Among those I worked with were Don Tyreman, of course, and Noel Wright who coined the phrase "Follow John" for a Conservative candidate seeking election to Parliament in a North Shore constituency. The phrase was taken over and employed nationally in support of the candidacy of party leader John Diefenbaker, who went on to become Prime Minister as described earlier. Noel went on to become the editor of the North Shore News, the community newspaper serving North and West Vancouver.

Audrey Benson was media buyer, Howard Bidwell, a financial guru was the treasurer and along the way I had a hand in the hiring of artist Doug Sandland who moved with wife Trudy from Seattle to become art director on the advertising side of the business.

I also renewed links with niece Karen Hembree, who worked with our O'Brien Consultants group for a time, before becoming a dental assistant with Dr. Stan Heinrichs, the Port Moody dentist who looked after our dental needs for more than a dozen years and was still fixing my teeth as 2018 ended.

We had stayed with Karen, her brother Richard, and her parents — Jean's brother David and wife Edith. David died in 1985. Jean and I remained close with Edith for the next 27 years as she moved into Parkwood Manor retirement home, where she lived for several years with her sister Bert, then after Bert's passing well into her nineties, into residential care at Cartier House. Edith suffered dementia and died August 15, 2012 at age 98.

At the same time, we followed Dick's career from afar as he

took turns at teaching moguls skiing, creating interesting art work through his brief involvement with painting, then acquiring an engineer ticket from Lakehead University in Thunder Bay and grabbing a full-page photo and story in August 1989 in People magazine. Our family still displays half a dozen of his paintings on walls of our homes. I purchased them for a few hundred dollars to help Dick with his university expenses.

The People story and photo recognized Dick's role in the development of what the magazine described as "a seven-pound device with the appropriate name of Survivor". The device was credited with saving the lives of shipwreck survivors William and Simone Butler, a couple from Miami. Simone, 52, said without the device "we'd be dead today. They survived 66 days before being rescued by the Costa Rican Coast Guard.

> People reported: "The Butlers' ordeal began on June 15, two months into their round-the-world sail, their 40-foot yacht was attacked and sunk by whales some 1,200 miles off Costa Rica. Scrambling into their rubber raft, they barely had time to grab a little food, some fishing gear and the Survivor 35, which is a manually operated pump for converting saltwater to fresh. For more than two months they subsisted mostly on raw fish and a precious three litres of potable water that William Butler, 60, squeezed out of the Survivor each day."

The People article said "the principle behind the Survivor was not new; it's a process called reverse osmosis in which brackish water is forced through a semipermeable membrane that blocks the salt but passes the liquid. "In the past, however, all such systems were huge, motorized devices pumping at 1,000 pounds per square inch. And all were clearly impractical for lifeboat use."

Dick Hembree, then 36 and with Recovery Engineering in Minneapolis, inspired by a prototype started by a fellow Minneapolis engineer named Bill Warner, completed a novel design: an easily portable desalination pump that could be hand operated by a single person. The article was accompanied by a two-third page photo of Dick with Brian Sullivan, Recovery Engineering's president, seated in a rowboat, toasting the life-saving pump – presumably with desalinated water in their glasses.

When Dick retired from Recovery Engineering, he was financially secure from his many successes in pump designs. The family settled in Bellingham, Washington to be near their friends and family in Vancouver without enduring Canadian taxation that would have been very costly had they returned to Canada at the time. In Bellingham, Dick indulged his interest in flying, purchasing a single-engine Cirrus aircraft with its own parachute. Jean and I flew with him to a Gulf Island for a lunch outing, then returned to Bellingham airport.

## 22

# A LOVE AFFAIR WITH HAWAII

When I left the O'Brien empire without another job confirmed, Jack Wasserman included in his widely read column in The Sun an item announcing that I was on the job market. Not long after that, I was introduced to Peter Downes, then Vice-President, Corporate Communications at Canada's largest forest company, MacMillan Bloedel, and accepted an opportunity to join his department as Manager, Special Projects.

My MB employment began May 1, 1972 and between the O'Brien departure and that date, I had a few weeks of relaxed independence. Jean, Ginny, Kerry, Peggi and I took advantage of that to start a long love affair with Hawaii. We travelled to Maui, stayed for nearly three weeks at the Maui Lu, developed by Gordon Gibson Sr., who I became acquainted with when he was a Liberal member of the B.C. legislature and I was covering the legislature for CP.

Gordon and his wife Louise acquired the Kihei property, near Kalepolepo Beach Park in 1956 for a reported $34,000. They built themselves a home there and in 1960 began building guest units to accommodate family and friends who came to visit.

The stories told at the time we were there said Gibson had ordered materials to build two or three guest bungalows but the shipment was much larger than anticipated. As a result, many more units were built and rentals became available to the public.

Our 1972 visit coincided with a stay by a plane load of Inuit from the North West Territories on a tour led by Pat Carney, a journalist I worked alongside when she was with The Province in Vancouver. She later was elected to Parliament, became a Cabinet Minister in the Mulroney government and still later a Senator.

We enjoyed the opportunity to meet these fellow Canadians, party with them and share in the fun events that went on at the Maui Lu. It didn't take long to note the physical similarities between the Inuit and the locals. After the visiting Inuit had a few days to accumulate Hawaii-style clothing, we found it difficult to distinguish them from native Hawaiians!

The Maui Lu property had a giant Longhouse that served as dining room, bar and entertainment centre where Jesse Nakooka, who drove the bus that brought us from airport to the Maui Lu, led the entertainment, as pianist and vocalist. He went on to become a star among Hawaii's entertainers. There also was a nine-hole pitch and putt golf facility on the property – and we tanned there as well as on the beaches.

Enroute home, we wanted to experience Waikiki beach, so booked a couple of nights at the Illikai Hotel. On arrival, the hotel had given away the adjoining rooms we'd booked so with no increase in our cost, we were lodged in a two-bedroom suite on the 18$^{th}$ floor, overlooking the Pacific Ocean. The view was sensational, the space very comfortable for the five of us, but somehow the informality of the Maui Lu seemed much more friendly and relaxing.

We returned to Maui often over the years, staying again at the Maui Lu with Phyllis and Lyall Hawkins, neighbors and good friends from the Glenayre neighborhood in Port Moody. Then upgrading to a new facility named Hale Pau Hana, where at the time of our first residency there we could have bought a new one-

*Remember the Good Times*

bedroom beachfront condo for $25,000 U.S. We didn't take advantage, but we did rent there two or three more times.

On one week-long visit, we stayed in a superb two-bedroom duplex in a waterfront property named the Wailea Elua Village, whose entry gate was opposite a Wailea Golf Club fairway, a couple of kilometres beyond the Kihei boundary, on the main Maui highway leading to Makena. The place was owned by Don Graham, who had Canadian Tire outlets in B.C. and was an active member of the fund-raising committees of Science World.

He asked me to do some reworking of communications documents used by the property management to greet new arrivals, to soften the language. My fees for the work were reinvested in the rent for the week – representing a significant discount over what would have been the going rate at the time.

Jean and I enjoyed the luxury but found the residents not as warm and friendly as those at other places we'd stayed on Maui, including apartments at the Kihei Surfside, a six-storey development with a large tract of water-front property. A few steps across a parking lot took us to the same long, sandy beach at the waterfront side of the Don Graham's Wailea place. That beach invited walks in the morning sunshine and easy and fun snorkelling around the lava rock where the beach began in Kihei.

The rock extended around the water side of the Surfside's huge expanse of lawn and this provided great turtle watching from the lawn chairs. It also provided a spectacular backdrop to sunset cocktail hours where many new friendships developed among the visitors from many states in the U.S., provinces in Canada and overseas nations. At least three of our visits there coincided with Hallowe'en and the regular visitors dressed in costumes and partied hard in celebration.

We also visited Kuai on three trips to the Islands. We toured Maui, Oahu, Kuai and the big island of Hawaii on three cruises from Vancouver to Hawaii and return. The first, 17 days aboard Holland America's Zaandam came in April, 2007, and included a stop in Seattle on the way to Hawaii. The second also was aboard the Zaandam in April 2010. The third was aboard the HAL's Oosterdam in April 2012 and Dan and Carolyn McArdle joined us on this one. The four of us took a day-long tour of the Big Island to view volcanos and many other popular sites.

Our latest and last visit to Hawaii came at the end of 2015 when, as guests of our daughter, Kerry, the entire family – 13 of us in total – spent 14 days at Turtle Bay, on the North Shore of Oahu, watching huge waves that attract the world's best surfers. Keegan was accompanied by husband Wes Lawrence, but that visit took place before Bryce had connected with Lisa Jorgensen, a criminal and regulatory lawyer in Toronto.

From her earliest years, Kerry seemed to have a strong sense of independence. Like her sisters, she was competitive, in school studies, athletics and virtually everything she put her hand and mind to. In 1974 she graduated from Grade 8 at Banting Junior Secondary, earning recognition as the top Academic student and still has a table-top inscribed copy of The Golden Encyclopedia of Music to prove it.

She was a straight "A" student throughout her years at Port Moody Senior Secondary, where she achieved a rare triple in her final year. She won the PMSS Trustees' Award for top academic student in the graduating class of 1978, the Sportswoman of the Year award for top female athlete and the Phoenix Club Award in recognition of outstanding achievement in community service, academics and athletics.

She also earned an employee dependent scholarship in the 1978-79 school year from BC Tel while I was Public Affairs Director there. With no prompting from me, she then enrolled in the Faculty of Arts at Carlton University in Ottawa, majoring in journalism and French. She also earned a spot on the varsity volleyball team.

After one term, she decided to take a whole new approach to her life, returned to Vancouver, found employment in the financial world and began a five-year study program to earn her Certified General Accountant (CGA) ticket. I know first hand of her

*Remember the Good Times*

diligence in that study because each week on my way to work I delivered her study paper to the CGA office in Vancouver.

When Peggi chose to mark her 40$^{th}$ birthday in 2002 by running the Chicago Marines marathon, Kerry joined her in training and they both ran the 40 kms successfully. It was the start of a career of running for Kerry, who later added cycling and swimming to her athletic endeavors.

Over the years, she participated in many marathons in Chicago, New York, California and Hawaii and she qualified for the April 2005 Boston Marathon, the first of several she ran. She did triathlons – swimming, bicycling and running — in the Okanagan in British Columbia; swam from Alcatraz to shore in San Francisco; and cycled often in France and Italy on organized vacation tours set up by Butterfield and Robinson travel service. She also cycled in the Carolinas with friends from Toronto.

She began her financial career with Canada Trust; worked closely with its CEO Ed Clark at the time of the Toronto Dominion Bank merger with Canada Trust; and while filling all the job requirements earned an MBA from the University of Western Ontario in London. She advanced in the TD Bank group to Executive Vice-President.

On November 30, 2009, Kerry was feted as one of Canada's most powerful women at a gala in Toronto where the Women's Executive Network (WXN) toasted those named to its seventh annual Top 100 list. The special Globe & Mail "Report on Top 100 Women" described the honorees as leaders in a wide range of fields. They were selected by an independent advisory board. Kerry was at that time Executive Vice-President, branch banking TD Canada Trust, TD Bank, Toronto and was chosen in the Corporate Executives category. She made the Top 100 list twice more and became a member of the Top 100 Hall of Fame.

Generous to a fault, she invited Jean and me to join her on some of her travels. One of the most exciting and memorable trips from October 26 to November 8, 2006 took us to Toronto, then with Kerry to an overnight in Bogota, Columbia, a couple of

JIM PEACOCK

nights in Quito, Ecuador and an 11-day cruise aboard the Isabella with 26 passengers touring the Galapogos Islands.

When Jean and I sailed aboard the Eurodam September 11, 2008 from Quebec City to New York, Kerry met us in NYC and hosted a unique dinner in honor of Jean's 79th birthday. We dined at the Asiate in the Mandarin Oriental Hotel at Columbus circle, overlooking Central Park from the 35th floor.

All of the family were treated to tickets to many of the 2010 Winter Olympic Games held in Vancouver and Whistler and, as noted earlier, she purchased for me my silver medal – a 2010 Chevrolet Equinox that had been a part of the vehicle fleet serving the Games.

*On the beach at a Club Med gathering hosted by Kerry in Mexico the family – l to r – Jean Jim, Ginny, Kerry and Peggi*

In March 2010, the whole family spent ten days at Club Med, Punta Cana, Dominican Republic to celebrate Kerry's 50th birthday. And it was a family affair again in December 2011 when we spent seven nights at Club Med, Ixtapa, Mexico to mark our 60th wedding anniversary.

## 23

## B.C. TELEPHONE COMPANY MY FIRST PR CLIENT

My first O'Brien Consultants' assignment was to assist BC Tel management with media relations during a lengthy public hearing called by the Canadian Transport Commission, the Federal regulatory agency then overseeing BC Tel, the telephone company operating throughout most of British Columbia.

It was one of several regional monopolies – in Alberta it was AGT, for Alberta Government Telephones until AGT was privatized and became TELUS — providing phone services when competition was not permitted in this industry in Canada. That changed in 1985 when the regulator allowed competition in long distance services and changed significantly with the introduction of cell phone services in the 1990s.

In any event, these monopolies were subject to regulation to protect consumers. As a national company, BC Tel was subject to Federal regulation, at that time by the Federal Transport Commission.

BC Tel had not had a rate increase in several years, nor was it seeking one then. The regulator simply decided to examine the company's rates, operations, practices and policies, so ordered the hearings.

J. Ernest Richardson had recently moved from Nova Scotia to become BC Tel's Chief Executive Officer. His team included Vice-Presidents of Finance, Operations, Engineering, Marketing, Labor Relations and other business segments and each one prepared evidence to be presented to the Commission at the hearings taking place in Vancouver.

For weeks in advance of the start of these hearings, I worked with the Vice-Presidents, legal counsel and others, drafting news releases focusing on positive elements of their evidence. Some of it was highly technical; I rewrote and edited the news release summaries as I would have done as a CP reporter; the only difference being that I checked back with the person who had prepared the evidence to ensure my interpretations were accurate.

When the hearing began, BC Tel's witnesses were on the stand for ten sitting days without cross examination. The news materials I had prepared were accepted by media covering the sessions, I believe largely because those reporters knew my background and had trust in the accuracy and objectivity of the summaries. In any event, for two weeks, daily media across B.C. were publishing and broadcasting positive news about BC Tel.

David Barrett, the former NDP Premier, made a presentation during the third week of the hearing. By that time media interest had waned; I played reporter, wrote a news report of what Barrett had to say and provided it in timely fashion to the CP Vancouver news desk. A CP editor put the Vancouver (CP) dateline on it and sent it out to CP's broadcast and print clients, many of whom published it verbatim.

The results achieved during this hearing put the O'Brien agencies and Michael O'Brien himself in good standing for a long time, particularly with Ernie Richardson. Michael and I later participated in Richardson tours of various areas of the province, where he met with employees at work and at special events. At the same time, as one of few CEOs to visit the rural areas of

*Remember the Good Times*

British Columbia, and taking time to have lunch or perhaps a coffee with local news editors and reporters, he made a highly positive contribution to the image of BC Tel and its leadership.

He also supported BC Tel's involvement in community development, including an O'Brien-agency-recommended financial grant to the Vancouver Aquarium to help it build a dolphin pool at its Stanley Park location, an activity that led to working with the Aquarium's long-time director Murray Newman.

My activities expanded to include preparing speaking notes for the CEO, preparing text for the company's annual report to shareholders, assisting with employee communications, helping to publicize new service offerings and financial results, and the preparation of copy for public information advertising.

One memorable ad I created in 1968 helped BC Tel convince its own employees that it was on to a good idea when its safety people decided vehicle drivers should place brightly-colored traffic cones in front of and at the rear of the vehicle and do a walk around to make sure the driver didn't accidentally run over something or someone.

Our youngest daughter, Peggi, was five years old. We set up a photo of her on her tricycle behind a BC Tel van. The driver was placing a cone at the rear of the van. The headline on this ad read: HER CONE IS FOR ICE CREAM; OUR CONES ARE FOR HER SAFETY This text, starting with a sub-heading, ran below the heading:

"Service with safety is the B.C.Telephone Company's objective and cones help us meet it.

The B.C.Telephone Company has more than 1,500 vehicles on the road to help bring telephone services to the people of British Columbia.

These vehicles come in a variety of sizes and shapes. And we know from experience that they often attract a lot of interest, especially among curious youngsters like Peggi, the five-year-old ice cream eater pictured above.

We at B.C. Telephone are keenly interested in her safety and that of all youngsters, just as we are keenly interested in the safety of all British Columbians. That's why we take special care to train our vehicle operators in safe driving and to provide practices designed to prevent accidents.

One of the safety practices we've adopted is called the "cone method of circle check." It requires that each of our vehicles carry cones of bright red color and that each driver place one in front of his vehicle and another behind it when it is parked. That's what installer-repairman Percy Johnson is doing in the photo above. Before he moves his truck, he'll walk to the front and from there to the back to pick up the cones. As he circles the vehicle, he'll become aware of objects around it – including any youngsters who may be nearby.

In this way, he prevents accidents in which it is so easy to harm such things as bicycles, tricycles, children's toys — and ice-cream-eating youngsters with incurable curiosity.

B.C. Telephone's more than 7,200 employees strive constantly to provide good telephone service. They also strive to do so in complete safety for all concerned.

Our objective is service with safety and the cone method of circle check for vehicles is just one more way we meet it.

This safety practice has continued at BC Tel ever since and has been adopted by many others with vehicle fleets on the road.

Work on the BC Tel account brought me in touch with some interesting people, among them Faye Leung. When I met her, she was active in a Vancouver Chinatown organization that worked with BC Tel in having telephone booths styled like Pagodas placed at strategic locations in the downtown Chinatown neighborhood. I helped publicize the locations.

Over the years that followed, our paths crossed several times through mutual involvement in community events, including annual Chinatown New Year's parades in which politicians of all stripes marched. The last business card she gave me billed her as Honorary Consul General of Guyana, a Member of the British Commonwealth, with this subhead "for the Government of Guyana to the People's Republic of China and to the Far East."

## 24

## SPONSORSHIP OF NANCY GREENE

### PORTRAYED A POSITIVE LIFESTYLE

Nancy Greene, born in Ottawa May 11, 1943 but raised in Rossland, B.C. where she began skiing on Red Mountain in British Columbia's West Kootenay region, earned a place in history as one of the best known Canadian skiers.

Nancy and her two sisters and three brothers all skied from the age of three. Her father and mother were both avid skiers and founding members of the Red Mountain Ski Club. Nancy began ski racing in high school. She was inspired by Lucille Wheeler of St. Jovite, Quebec who became the first Canadian to win an Olympic medal – the bronze at the 1958 Cortina Winter Olympics.

Wheeler also won two gold medals at that year's World Championships and Nancy won her first trophy, placing second to her sister in the Canadian Junior Championships. After rooming with Anne Heggtveit of Ottawa at the 1960 Squaw Valley Olympics where Anne won gold in slalom, Nancy was determined to win an Olympic gold medal.

In nine years of ski racing, Greene won three U.S. championships, nine Canadian titles, and the inaugural 1967 World Cup

## JIM PEACOCK

over-all Alpine title. She finished seventh in the downhill at the 1964 Innsbruck Olympic Winter Games. The 1968 Grenoble Olympic Winter Games marked her third Olympics competition. She finished tenth in the downhill, then won silver in the slalom.

Her last chance for a gold in Grenoble was the giant slalom in which she skied a near-perfect race, and after a timing clock malfunction was corrected she won by 2.68 seconds, the largest margin in the event's history. She then put together a string of victories in all three alpine events and handily won her second over-all World Cup title. In two years of World Cup competition she won 13 times.

Then she retired from amateur racing at the age of 24 and began a successful professional career. The first contract she accepted was an assignment for the B.C. Telephone Company. BC Tel's CEO Ernie Richardson had teenaged daughters at that time and a parental concern about the drug culture that was impacting many young people.

Greene, having achieved world-wide recognition through her skiing success, was a positive role model. Richardson supported the idea that BC Tel and the community it served would both benefit from a sponsorship that brought Greene's leadership to teenagers through direct communication at high school and other public appearances and indirect messaging through media coverage of this communication.

I was given the opportunity to negotiate the sponsorhip agreement with Nancy and her then agent Doug Maxwell and subsequently to work on media relations to spread what Nancy told the audiences she addressed. One of her appearances was at the high school in Cranbrook, B.C., a couple of hundred kilometres east of her home town of Rossland.

I picked her up at her home at 5 a.m. and she dozed in the car during the drive to Cranbrook. There, she told an enthralled audience that skiing, in training and competition, brought her "highs" that couldn't be achieved through drug impairment; that athletics could help to build respect, self-confidence and strong personal development with long-standing individual benefits. She delivered that message face-to-face with people of all ages who came to see her at the BC Tel booth at the Pacific National Exhibition in Vancouver that fall.

*Nancy Greene became an honorary member of The Timber Club, Hotel Vancouver ceremony with maitre'd Pierre, Michael O'Brien, left, Jim Peacock and Don Tyreman.*

I was fortunate enough to be a part of a brief ritual with Nancy when she was presented with a hard hat and joined many of the city's prominent forest industry executives as an honorary member of the then popular restaurant, the Timber Club, in the Hotel Vancouver. My Photo collection includes one showing Mickey O'Brien, Nancy in a Cowichan knit sweater, me and Don Tyreman at a table in the Timber Club dining room while Pierre, the maitre'd waits to place a Timber Club hard hat on Nancy's head.

In 1968, Nancy served on Prime Minister Pierre Elliott

JIM PEACOCK

Trudeau's "Task Force of Sports" and assisted the Canadian Ski Team with fund-raising and promotion. In that work she met Al Raine, then the new program director of Canada's National Ski Team. They were married in April 1969. Their twin sons were born in Montreal in 1970. Their involvement in ski industry development in Whistler and Sun Peaks is widely known. In 1999, she and Wayne Gretsky were chosen Canada's female and male Athletes of the year.

## 25

## MARY MCLUHAN AND TEACHER AWARDS

Among the people I worked with at BC Tel was James MacInnes, Vice-President Marketing. Through that link I was introduced to Mary McLuhan, daughter of Marshall McLuhan, the eminent Canadian scholar, social critic and futurist who died in 1980. She convinced Jim and BC Tel to become a sponsor in British Columbia of the Marshall McLuhan Distinguished Teacher Awards Canada. Jim asked me to work with Mary on the awards program.

I coordinated and publicized the 1988, the 1989-90 and the 1991-92 awards programs and have a hand-written note signed by Mary saying: "To Jim: for making the 1990 Awards program such a major success."

On Dec. 8, 1988 in the Expo 86 Discovery Theatre, ten teachers from elementary and secondary schools in nine different B.C. communities were honored as the B.C. winners in that year's Canada Program of the Marshall McLuhan Distinguished Teacher Awards.

The awards were a presentation of the McLuhan Centre, a non-profit educational centre established by Mary to honour the memory and further the work of her father, who studied the effects of mass media on thought and behaviour and became famous in the 1960s for such things as coining the phrase "the medium is the message."

The B.C. Award winners were chosen by a special committee chaired by Charles J. Connaghan, chairman of Premier Vander Zalm's Roundtable on the Environment. Other committee members were John R. Fleming, assistant deputy minister, educational programs, Ministry of Education; Douglas Hoover program director, CKVU television; Michael Lombardi, Second Vice-President, B.C. Teachers Federation; Malcolm McTavish, Education Consultant, Apple Canada Inc.; Donna Mackey, a former high school teacher and a member of the board of the Open Learning Agency; Lucille Pacey, vice-president of the Open Learning Agency; Darlene Poole, a communications consultant; and Dr. Stanley Shapson, associate dean of education, Simon Fraser University.

The Master of Ceremonies was Patrick Reid of Expo 86 fame. McLuhan's widow Corrine and daughter Mary were among the dignitaries on hand, along with the Hon. David Lamb, Lieutenant Governor of B.C. and the B.C Education Minister Hon. Tony Brummet.

The presenters included Dr. Howard Petch, President, University of Victoria; Colin Patterson, Vice-President Corporate Development, B.C. Telephone Company; Elsie Murphy, President, B.C. Teachers Federation; Rick Hansen; T.J. Hearn, Vice-President, Retail Department, Esso Petroleum Canada; Dr. Daniel Birch, Vice-President, Academic & Provost, University of B.C.; Dr. William Leiss, Professor, Department of Communications, Simon Fraser University; Stuart H. Noble, President and Chief Operating Officer, Pacific Press; Lui Passaglia, B.C. Lions; and author Peter C. Newman.

The Minister of Education presented s cheque for $2,500 and the Lieutenant Governor presented a McLuhan Medal to each winner.

*Remember the Good Times*

For the record, the 1988 winners were David Allan, Mangold Elementary, Victoria; Anand S. Atal, Burnaby South Sr. Secondary; . Christopher Bowers, Prince of Wales Secondary, Vancouver; Dean W. Dogherty, G.F. Strong Program, Vancouver; Barbara Keating, Richard McBride Elementary, New Westminster; Michael C. Malfesi, Garibaldi Secondary, Maple Ridge; Greig McArthur, D.W. Poppy Secondary, Langley; Ken McClean, Beaver Valley Secondary, Fruitvale; Gerry R. Morgan, Windermere School District Invermere; and Thomas A. Tylka, Vancouver School Board.

The screening committee for the 1989-90 awards was again chaired by Chuck Connaghan with other members including John R. Fleming, Donna Mackey, Lucille Pacey, Darlene Poole and Dr. Stanley Shapson.

The presentation ceremony, held at the Expo 86 site's B.C. Club, was hosted by Education Minister Brummet, the MC was Chris Hebb of CKVU Television, and presenters were James Cameron of Telecom Canada, Stuart Noble of Southam Inc.; Bruce Telford of Xerox Canada, Chuck Cote of K Mart Canada Ltd. and Bernadette Cartwright of Volkswagen Canada.

The winners were four teachers from Marigold Elementary in Victoria — David Bird, Doug Wilson, Steve Hambleton and team leader, 1988 McLuhan winner David Allan; Chuck Heath, Ridgeway Elementary, North Vancouver; David Sharp, J. Alfred Laird Elementary, Invermere; Mary Short, Uplands Elementary, Langley; and Graeme Wilson, Rosedale Secondary, Rosedale.

The screening committee changed for the 1991-1992 Awards. Lucille Pacey was its chair; Other Members were Orest Kruhlak Executive Director, the Laurier Institute; Barbara Stewart, Past President of the Variety Club of B.C.; Prof. Phil Winne of the Faculty of Education at Simon Fraser University; David Williams, Director of Program Support Services in the B.C.Ministry of Education, and Robert A. Worcester, Chair, Department of Psychology, Vancouver Community College.

JIM PEACOCK

I served as Master of ceremonies at the presentation of these awards at the Empress Hotel in Victoria on Feb. 18, 1992. The Awards and McLuhan Medals were presented to the following winners:

Brent Cameron, Wondertree Learning Centre, Vancouver; Susan Crichton, Lucerne Elementary Secondary, New Denver; Kevin Harrison, Caruhu Sr. Secondary School, Campbell River; Carol Marshall/David Allan, Marigold Elementary, Victoria and Bryan Stovell, Nanaimo District Secondary. (Of note, one of Bryan Stovell's music students was jazz pianist and singer Diane Krall.)

## 26

# VARIETY CLUB AND A NEW CHILDREN'S HOSPITAL

BC Tel's Advertising Manager Bryan Holliday and Employee Communications Manager Keith Matthews were active volunteers with the Variety Club of Western Canada, later the Variety Club of B.C. and later still Variety, The Children's Charity. They encouraged me to get involved, too, and I did. I helped to publicize Variety Club's activities through media relations activities and preparation of literature, participated in fund-raising golf tournaments, both as a player and as an organizer, and volunteered during telethons and other activities.

A lot of time went into this volunteer work and there are many details that don't warrant inclusion here. One detail had significant impact on my involvement with the club and with Variety's major projects. By this time I had departed the O'Brien organization and joined MacMillan Bloedel's Corporate Communications team led by Vice-President Peter Downes.

Late in 1973, Irv Levenson was in line to take over the Chief Barker (President) role with Tent 47. He developed a heart condition and had to stand aside to recover. I was asked to step in for the 1974 term and reluctantly did so.

JIM PEACOCK

In that role, I had prominent parts in the 1974 Variety Telethon on BCTV and a subsequent Heart Awards Dinner. My souvenirs from this time include photos with actor and Star Wars star Leonard Nemoy, Country Singer Blake Edmonds, and Bob McGrath of Sesame Street fame.

*L to R Big Bird and Bob McGrath of Sesame Street, Aussie Rolph Harris, Chief Barker Jim Peacock, Leonard Nemoy of Star Wars, Singer Blake Emonds, Variety International Vice-Preident Peter Barnett at 1974 telethon.*

In 1975, as the Chairman of the Board of Tent 47, the Variety Club of BC (which even then was THE Children's Charity!), I was given the task of identifying the next major project to be funded by the Variety Club.

Tent 47 was formed in 1965 for the purpose of raising funds and employing them to promote the welfare, health and well-being of children in British Columbia. By 1979, with the support of its media partners and of British Columbians, it had raised $7.5 million and funded three major projects:

**1. Variety Farm Training Centre**, a $600,000 facility in Ladner with five residence complexes accommodating 44 students plus a variety of other buildings and facilities where youths with mental disorders were given training in agricultural work. In 1974, in partnership with the B.C. and Yukon Building Construction Trades Council and the Amalgamated Construction Association of B.C., $100,000 was invested to add Unity House to provide training in construction work. Over the years, many graduated and went on to productive jobs.

**2. Variety's Treatment Centre for Children**, in Surrey, another $600,000 was invested in a facility operated by the Lower Fraser Valley Cerebral Palsy Association to treat children up to age 15 who have a condition of cerebral palsy or associated ailments. Opened in 1974 to replace an inadequate and overcrowded building, it was expanded in 1977 wirh hydrotherapy pool, physiotherapy gymnasium, kindergarten training rooms and occupational therapy facilities. Its case load soon grew to 300 from 170.

3. **Variety Club's Bob Berwick Memorial Centre,** built on the campus of the University of B.C. as the new home of the B.C. Mental Retardation Institute. The BCMRI provided development and treatment programs for children up to age eight and had about 40 youngsters enrolled in its special pre-school, many groups aged 10 months to three years using its unique Bill Galt Memorial hydrotherapy pool (named for the late Vancouver Sun Managing Editor) and some 1,500 to 2,000 visitors a year. The $1 million centre (named for the late architect Bob Berwick, who as a Variety member was involved in design of many of the facilities it funded) also offered training to university students.

With these successes, – plus having raised resources to assist some 50 other beneficiaries and put some 60 special buses, called

Sunshine Coaches, on the road to transport children served by other organizations, and with the continued support of what then was BCTV (and the Vancouver Sun), we on the Board had some confidence we could take on something big for kids in B.C.

At the suggestion of Vancouver Sun columnist Jack Wasserman, two of the leading pediatricians in the province — Dr. Sydney Israels and Dr. Geoff Robinson — invited me to tour an outpatient service for kids that was in an old house on West 10th, many kilometres away from the then existing Children's Hospital on West 59th. Dr. Israels reminded me many times after that tour and a lunch discussion "there's no such thing as a free lunch".

I recommended to the Variety Club that we commit to raise $1 million to build a new facility for outpatient treatment of kids. There's a whole book full of political details inbetween, but to cut to the chase, when the government of the day changed in 1975, I wrote – on December 12, 1975 — to the incoming premier, Bill Bennett, to advise that the Variety Club was ready — with the BCTV telethon support — to raise $1 million for that outpatient facility for Children's Hospital.

As requested, Premier Bennett asked his first Health Minister, Bob McClelland, to contact us. The Minister of Health did so on December 30, 1975 and set Friday, January 23, 1976 as a meeting date. Keith Matthews and I attended that meeting which started a process that led to the construction of a new Children's Hospital at the Shaughnessy Hospital site on Oak Street in Vancouver, complete with a diagnostic centre.

The response of Premier Bennett and his government was in sharp contrast to that of Premier David Barrett and Health Minister Dennis Cocke of the short-lived NDP government defeated in 1975 after three years in office. My files contain letters dated Sept.10 and Sept. 26, 1975. The first outlined what my committee was recommending to the Tent 47 Crew in terms of funding a new diagnostic centre. The second advised him that the Crew had unanimously endorsed the recommendation to raise $1 million toward that project.

*Remember the Good Times*

We sought assurance that the government would approve of Children's Hospital proceeding with it. Neither letter brought a response and when I sent copies of the correspondence to Premier Barrett's attention, I received only an acknowledgement from an aide that my letter had been received and would be brought to the premier's attention.

In the end, the Variety Club committed to raise $5 million (again, with BCTV's support) and the provincial government agreed to put up the rest of the $35 million to build what became BC's Children's Hospital. It took time.

Dr. Israels, who had come to B.C. from Winnipeg 15 years before our lunch date with the promise that a new Children's Hospital would be built, didn't survive long enough to see his dream come true. He died suddenly July 17, 1978 at the age of 63 while at the old Children's Hospital discussing better medical facilities. But he knew it was happening! He had attended the sod turning for the new Children's Hospital on Nov. 15, 1977.

Over the years, I have been very proud of the role I was able to play as a catalyst in getting this hospital built. Three of our four grandchildren were born there. And Children's became a big element of my business relationships as a public relations practitioner, in part because of the Ronald McDonald House relationship with the hospital and my involvement with McDonald's as a client. That began in 1986 and was related directly to Expo 86.

During my Variety Club activities, I often met famed band leader Dal Richards, who led his orchestra in telethon performances even when he was employed by the Variety Club in an administrative post. Later in our relationship, I recommended him to the operators of a retirement residence called Terraces on 7$^{th}$ Avenue, just west of Granville Street in Vancouver, as a person who could help their sales promotion. Dal did so, putting on afternoon tea dances in the Terrace's dining room and speaking on their behalf in TV commercials. Dal lost his first wife, singer Lorraine McAllister, in 1984 after 32 years together. In 2001, he married Muriel Honey, the ex-wife of radio broadcaster Rick

Honey who I also knew from PR promotions and his frequent involvement in McDonald's McHappy Days. Dal Richards died on New Year's Eve, 2015 at age 97.

## 27

## MACMILLAN BLOEDEL PLACE AND OTHER FUN THINGS

On my departure from O'Brien Consultants, I received this note from J. Ernest Richardson, President and CEO of BC Tel: "While our relationship will not be as close as in the past, I do hope that we can keep our friendship." It was dated April 17, 1972. We did keep our friendship. And our paths crossed again when Richardson became the Chairman of MacMillan Bloedel.

I also served B.C. Tel communications needs again, albeit after a break that lasted five years. Following my seven years with O'Brien and our first Hawaiian vacation, I spent five years as manager, special communications projects with MacMIlan Bloedel, then Canada's largest forest company.

I joined MB in 1972 – and some of my special projects were very special. For example: MacMillan Bloedel Place – A Walk In The Forest which, in an August 31, 1976 article the Vancouver Sun headline described as "New museum final word on forestry." Keane Lipinski's article read:

> Want an instant education in Forestry? Go to the new MacMillan Bloedel Place tucked away in the northeast corner of Van Dusen

JIM PEACOCK

Garden. In the museum, which opened officially today, can be found displays on almost every aspect of forestry in an indoor setting of running creeks with native and semi-tropical plants.

The centre is designed to blend in with its surroundings on a 3.5-acre site. Set into a hillside, its roof is covered with plants. A 12-foot waterfall at its doorstep feeds the lake that borders its glass front wall. Although billed as "a walk in the forest" the building is actually an ultra-modern science museum with design and fabrication of the exhibits by Exhibitgroup Los Angeles Inc. – the same group which designed the Jacques Cousteau Living Sea display on board the Queen Mary in Long Beach, California.

"We asked them to design a museum with things people could do," said Jim Peacock, project manager. And there's lots to do. Visitors can press buttons and see slide presentations explaining dozens of aspects of plant growth and forest regeneration. There are quizzes to test visitors on what they learned about plant identification during the tour. Peacock said the museum is designed to appeal to the public of all ages, but that he expects many of them to be students. "We've got things we think will occupy young children," he said, pointing out a display where model birds and bees demonstrate pollination.

Some displays will appeal to forestry students, like one that consists of photographs of various forest soil types with the technical names attached. Then there is the theatre. Peacock said it seats 50 and has a library of nature films by Tommy Tompkins. One of the more academic displays is a map of the biogeoclimatic zones in B.C. designed by Dr. Vladimir Krajina, an honorary professor of botany at the University of British Columbia.

The staff of the museum will provide for the poor student who wishes to use the facilities but can't pay the cover charge to get into the gardens. "I think he can make a phone call and there'll be no trouble getting him in," said Peacock. MacMillan Bloedel spent about $500,000 on the project which entered the planning stages in May, 1973, he said. The museum employs four persons, including naturalist John Clark.

The lead up to the opening of MB Place began with internal discussion of the benefits of investing in education of the public in British Columbia. Peter Downes had been a leader in such things for some time, employing print and broadcast media to explain the forests as a renewable resource and to demonstrate that MB was a knowledgeable and responsible custodian of forest lands it harvested and replanted. W.J. VanDusen, for whom the botanical garden on what once was a golf course in Vancouver was named, had been Chief Forester in one of the predecessor companies that now made up MB.

There seemed to be value in the notion that a forestry education centre in a botanical garden in the heart of Vancouver would contribute to retention of public consent for MB to continue with its business. Downes was able to convince the budgeting authorities that it was worth exploring. That set the wheels in motion for development of a concept, exploring with the Van Dusen Garden authorities what might be possible, developing a presentation for Vancouver City Council, working with architects, builders, botanical experts and exhibit creators.

Peter Downes and I appeared before City Council, committed MB to paying the costs for the project – about $1.5 million for the design and construction of the building, about $500,000 for the exhibits and $250,000 a year to staff and maintain MB Place when it began operation. Tapping the vast forest photo and film library MB had built up over the years was over and above all that.

I travelled to Tucson, Arizona to visit the Arizona-Sonora Desert Museum, a botanical garden and natural history museum founded in 1962 and to Los Angeles several times to meet with Gene Grahn of Exhibitgroup. And I visited often with Dr.

JIM PEACOCK

Vladimir Krajina at UBC to build my understanding of the botanical aspects of B.C.'s commercial forests.

MB's then Chief Forester, Grant Ainscoth, opened the door to my conversations with Dr. Krajina, who was hesitant at first. With some hard work, I was able to convince him that we at MB sought a partnership in which I would write text for exhibits and other presentations and would rewrite as often as necessary to satisfy us that readers and viewers could understand and to satisfy him that the material remained botanically accurate.

I also worked closely with architect Paul Merrick of Thompson, Berwick, Pratt and Partners on the building design and throughout construction by Halse-Martin Construction Ltd. and maintained close contact with Roy Forester, Van Dusen Garden Curator. When everything came into place to begin operations, MB logging crews found a giant Western Red Cedar log and placed it beside the MB Place entrance. There, on August 31, 1976, J. Ernest Richardson, as Chairman of MB, delivered remarks of welcome, as did Mayor Art Phillips of Vancouver, Parks Board Commissioner May Brown and President Dr. Frank Turnbull of the Vancouver Botanical Gardens Association.

The Grand Opening itself was left to W.J. Van Dusen. He wielded a red hot branding iron, the tip of which bore the M-shaped MacMIlan Bloedel logo and with protective gloves and a small assist from me he burned the logo into the centre of the giant log.

The unique opening day's printed program, on soft brown paper, with a cover page window that contained a seed from a Douglas fir, and with thin white paper illustrations of four of B.C.'s five main commercial species – western hemlock, western red cedar, Douglas fir and amabilis fir – (the fifth is spruce) carried this text:

"MacMillan Bloedel Place is the offspring of an idea which, like seed sown in fertile soil, germinated and grew. The idea was simple enough – to assure that information about the nature of

*Remember the Good Times*

British Columbia's greatest natural resource, its forests, would be a part of the presentations of a major Botanical garden in the centre of Western Canada's most populous urban area.

"The idea became a unique "walk in the forest" – a physical structure often described as a non-building which contains many exhibits providing opportunities to "see" inside the forest and inside the tree itself. Many people nurtured the idea which became MacMillan Bloedel Place, a building of unusual design and construction and a place of most lively presentations of botanical, biological, ecological and general forest information.

The exhibits combine words, illustrations, sounds and action in ways which stimulate not only the more serious students of natural sciences but also the visitors with only casual interest in botany or biology. They provide many things to do, see, hear and sense. Visitors turn on the sun to activate a demonstration of the process of photosynthesis. They make the wind blow in an illustration of how pollen is carried to cones, causing fertilization which leads to production of seed. They match leaves, bark and cones to test their own ability to recognize trees of major species native to British Columbia.

"On visitor command, leaves show their seasonal colours and the presentation explains why the colours change. By turning on the sun again, the visitors activate a demonstration of the flow of water and mineral salts up from the roots through the stem of a tree and the flow of carbohydrates down from the leaves. In one special walk, you can sense the silence of an over-mature forest and experience the sensation of being in the middle of a burning forest.

"Reproductions of paintings by J. Fenwick Lansdowne show many of the birds of British Columbia. True-to-life specimens of defoliating, parasitic and pollinating insects are displayed with illustrations of many of the province's animals. Even the electronic aura which surrounds plant leaves is a subject displayed in MacMillan Bloedel Place. From the animated illustration of the process of cell division and stereo views of magnified photos of the fibre composition of the inside of a tree stem to the actual specimens of seeds, preserved in jewel-like encasements, MacMillan Bloedel Place provides an exciting learning experience.

"It is a fascinating addition to community facilities in a province where 60 per cent of the land is forested, where the economy is heavily dependent upon the forest and where the majority of the people live and work in urban communities, half of them in the Greater Vancouver area where the Van Dusen Garden is situated."

## 28

# A GREAT TIME TO BE WITH MB'S PR TEAM

MacMillan Bloedel was a great company in which to be a part of the public relations team during the five years of my employment there. Peter Downes, the Vice-President in charge, had a strong background in the entire communications field, having headed a successful advertising agency in his past. He reported directly to J.V. Clyne, then the Chairman and Chief Executive Officer of MB. And the company was profitable so could afford to do some excellent work in research, community and employee relations, corporate advertising, sponsorships and other activities that helped get its positive stories to the public.

Ours was treated as the management function that evaluated public attitudes, identified policies and procedures with the public interest and planned and executed a program of action to earn public understanding and acceptance. This approach arose largely from the realization that business had entered an era in which its relations with those around it can determine not only whether it continues to operate at a profit but – in extreme cases – whether it continues to operate at all. Senior management at that time recognized this is particularly true of an industry that makes use of a natural resource – part of the public domain.

In my job, I had some responsibility for research into public attitudes and was the company's liaison with The Canadian Trend Report, founded by a very bright woman from California named Kristin Shannon. She had developed a unique news analysis technique to forecast public attitudes towards corporate developments and operations. The messages that stood out from this research were these: 1. In our democratic society, businesses operate only with public consent; 2. Effective performance and communication are essential to earn public consent.

Corporate Communications was about communication – and we emphasized in our relationships with those responsible for company policy and operational performance that what they did and how well they did it created the foundation for effective communication to achieve the ultimate goal of public consent.

Our approach was one of fact-based education, not propaganda, not ballyhoo. We acted as eyes and ears for top management in bringing to light conditions creating an unfavourable climate, sometimes acting as a company conscience, sometimes doing a little nagging. In an effective communications program, the integrity of management comes through clearly and corporate policies are identified with the public interest.

In one presentation I made on behalf of the department to company managers, I said – and I've always believed it to be true – attempts to brainwash the public don't work. No amount of effort and clever use of communications techniques can succeed permanently in creating favorable public attitudes unless the impressions conveyed do in fact reflect the true character of the company, its policies and its personnel.

We developed programs and projects to promote goodwill; make the company known as a responsible custodian of forest resources and a producer of quality products; a company comprised of good people to deal with and an asset to the community, province and nation; a leader in research, engineering and product development; and a company that serves equally well the interests of the pubic, the shareholders and the employees.

Under Peter Downes' leadership, and with the help of such talented people as writer Bill Force, advertising creative writer Tom Baird and the best photographers that could be hired, MB created print and broadcast advertisements that both earned kudos for their content and style and delivered factual information, consistently illustrated with film and photos to reinforce messages that research indicated the public did not understand and appreciate. This advertising focused on such things as MB's intensive forestry program, its conservation of wood through full utilization of trees harvested, the importance of the forest industry to Canada's economy and the company's place in the industry.

AT ONE POINT, MB embarked on production and airing of an extensive television series entitled "The Incredible Forest" – with twelve half-hour programs built around a basic theme of MB's position as a responsible custodian of forest resources. These were aired on a Vancouver TV station with no commercials and presented a fairly comprehensive picture of company operations and how they are conducted to the benefit of the public. Each of these films then was given wide showings to schools, employee and community groups, clubs and other organizations.

MB also made headlines through its acquisition of broadcast rights for such spectacular film properties as Heidi and its sponsorship of them on national TV, accompanied by corporate commercials produced as mini-documentaries about MB operations.

I had roles in preparing materials for many of the print ads, for many news announcements, for use by company people in speaking to a variety of audiences, in organizing and supervising photography by such outstanding photographers as Steve Wilson of Seattle and Jay Maisal of New York, and in preparation of editorial content for shareholder reports.

I also participated in on-location filming for TV spots and features explaining MB operations. One of the people I met in that role was Virginia Greene. She was assisting the film crew the first time we met but she went on to much greater things. She became one of B.C.'s most prominent and successful business women, in 2007 being appointed to head the Business Council of B.C. Among other achievements, she founded GoDirect Marketing, led the promotion of Expo 86 and was a deputy minister in the provincial government tourism department. She died December 2, 2010.

At MB, I had a hand in planning and execution of designs and production of user-friendly road signs to advise people of safe accessibility to MB forest lands. On roads into areas where harvesting had been completed and new forests were growing, a sign with a large green dot told drivers the logging road was open to public use. The common symbol for "stop" with large red octogon was employed on signs where active logging work made it unsafe for the public to travel and "yield" with its yellow triangle where public and forestry workers could safely share the roads.

The people producing these signs – on plywood made by an MB mill – prepared a special one and presented it to me. It had a green dot and lettering that said Always Open To The Public. I put it on display in my office. By that time, J.V. Clyne had retired as the company's CEO, but as chairman he maintained an office on the same floor as our department. His Executive Assistant Margaret Clark saw my sign and, as a joke, had it hung beside the door to Clyne's office. He got a great charge out of it, had it photographed and sent it out to many friends as a Christmas card with a note saying, to the effect, "this is how you get treated when you retire."

Among my assignments was managing MB's sponsorship of Tommy Tompkins, a former police officer who became known for his television and film work in the wilds of B.C. and in Canada's northern wilderness. The sponsorship made it possible for Tompkins to take his wildlife films and experience directly to a wide variety of audiences, including schools. It was a goodwill building program – not one that carried any MB commercial messages.

Tommy had built his reputation through appearances regularly on CBC Television, including a show called "This Land". His work chronicled animal life in remote regions of B.C. and the Yukon and documented Tompkins' own methods of survival and travel through wilderness areas as he spent spring and summer in the bush, alone, and often acting as his own wildlife cinematographer. It all led to development of a successful television special called "Tommy Tompkins: Bushman" aired on CBC television in 1970.

Then came his own program called "Tommy Tompkins Wildlife Country" a series of 13 half-hour programs that featured him as the outdoorsman and environmentalist that he was. It aired at various times on CBC from January to December, 1971 and again from February 1972 to June 1974. The show's executive producer was Ray Hazzan, the producer Denis Hargrave.

The Tompkins celebrity was brought to the company's attention by its then advertising manager, Terry McDowell. Through the MB sponsorship, Tommy was able to continue his filming trips to the wilds and to carry his experiences and his conservation messages to young audience throughout British Columbia, by some estimates to as many as 100,000 school children in a year.

As a policeman he had seen some of the worst of the drug scene in Vancouver, a lifestyle he did not enjoy. As a bushman, he not only captured wildlife in the wilds, but healed some of the mental wounds inflicted by his police work. He also met many aboriginals across British Columbia and he often told me that the patronizing treatment aboriginals received from the Federal Indian Affairs system of the time was creating way more problems than benefits.

JIM PEACOCK

In 1974, Tommy Tompkins was named a Member of the Order of Canada for his work in focusing awareness on the natural environment. In 1977, as I was preparing to leave MB, the company's contract was heading towards its December 31, 1978 end. Tommy was considering an assignment with the then provincial Ministry of Recreation. The sponsorship was picked up by B.C. Hydro, where a former MB colleague named Douglas Coupar had joined the public relations department.

In time, while under sponsorship by Alcan and living in Prince George, he and a close friend, Bill Hickman, were filming grizzly bears along the Copper River north of Terrace when Tommy became ill. "He managed to get himself back to hospital but he was in pretty bad shape," Hickman said. Tommy apparently suffered an aneurism and died in Terrace hospital, aged 69.

In notes I prepared for Peter Downes to cover steps to be taken to maintain continuity of my tasks once I left, these additional responsibilities were listed: Corporate literature, including a documents titled "About MB" and "MB in B.C." both of which were distributed publicly; booklets setting out financial and operating statistics and the employee dependent scholarship program; printed student literature and educational slide-illustrated shows describing the forest industry in B.C. for distribution to schools; printed recreational guide maps; MB Liaison with the public relations advisory group of the Employers Council of B.C.

A brief news item that appeared about the same time reported:

"J.A. Peacock of Vancouver has won a Gold Quill Award of excellence for a continuing external communications program and an award of merit for special print communication for MacMillan Bloedel. The award is the most prestigious in its field. The program is sponsored by the International Association of Business Communicators, an organization of 3,600 professionals from around the world. Entries came from the U.S., Canada, Europe, Asia and Africa.

And, in a hand-written note dated October 27, 1977, Peter Downes wrote:

*Dear Jim:*

*I would not want you to leave MB without my making mention of the outstanding job you have done for the Company while you have been here. You have made an enormous contribution to the Department and in my view, which I have expressed to a good many people, your departure is a very serious loss to the Company. B.C. Tel is very fortunate to obtain the services of a man who works as hard as you do, whose counsel is so sound and whose integrity so total. I am proud to have worked with you Jim and I wish you great success and happiness in your new undertaking.*

*Sincerely, Peter*

## 29

# PARTY GROUP WAS NICKNAMED ADVERTISING OLD FARTS

During my time with MB, I became a part of a group comprised of advertising, public relations, media and related occupations who marked the run-up to Christmas each December with a Chinese lunch largely fueled by martinis. It was an offshoot of regular lunch outings with Peter Downes, his buddy Alan Black, a news media entrepreneur; George MacFarlane and Terry McDowell. Those often took place at the Timber Club in the Hotel Vancouver and at The Only Fish on East Hastings Street.

The Chinese restaurant that became the December luncheon site for several years was on West 41$^{st}$ Avenue in Kerrisdale and was called Hennesy's. I remember the food as outstanding. The martinis were mixed in large pitchers and the owner-operator kept pouring. Taxis or designated drivers back to work or home were the order of the day.

*Alan Black, Peter Downes and Jim*

JIM PEACOCK

Over the years, most of the community's senior advertising and public relations people, as well as media and printing industry people showed up – among them advertising legends Tom Baird, Dougald Lamb, Frank Palmer, Frank Anfield, Bob Bryant, Steve Vrlak and Alvin Wasserman; community newspaper ad rep Francois Freyvogel, broadcast star and Rock'n'Roll Hall of Famer Red Robinson; PR gurus David Brown, Gary Duke, Jim Gilmore, Doug Heal, John Kenmuir, Hal Holden, Dave Laundy, Jim McKeachie, Frank Walden, George MacFarlane, Jim MacInnes, Bob Johnson; Photographer Art Jones who launched BCTV (now Global), and Gary Fulton. Other attendees included Clare MacSorely, Fred Jenson and one-time Province Publisher Gerry Haslam.

After Peter Downes died in 1996, the venue for the event moved to the Shaughnessy Golf Club where Doug Lamb, Francois Freyvogel, Bryan Holliday and I were the organizers for several years, with help from Susan Kirkonnel. Sue and Dougald Lamb's long-time friend Betty were the only women who attended this event over the long haul but in the final two years, Susan brought along Maureen Giefing, who had worked at Lovick's and at the Vancouver Foundation.

The last lunch was held at Shaughnessy Golf Club in December, 2013. On November 20, 2014, Susan sent an e-mail to everyone on the foregoing list to say that "after speaking with a number of people who made it to the lunch last year about whether we should proceed with the event, we have decided that we should go out on a high – I think last year's get-together was one of the best (in recent memory). It was fun while it lasted and I really hope our paths will cross again along the way." Sadly, there was no 2014 Advertising Old Farts event and there has been none since.

## 30

## WHAT THE PUBLIC SEES MUST BE THE REAL THING

Early on in my MB assignment, I was privileged to represent my boss – Peter Downes – before an audience attending a May 3, 1977 Business/Industrial Advertising seminar organized by the Association of Canadian Advertisers at the Royal York Hotel in Toronto. Peter had been invited to describe the success of MB's use of advertising time and space in telling the company's corporate story.

Developments since then have changed our media scene world-wide. But on re-reading the notes prepared for that presentation, I've concluded that the premise upon which MB's corporate advertising was founded has currency even with social media added to today's mix of radio, TV and print, including newspapers and magazines.

MB used paid space – advertising – as one of many tools in its total communications program. It also did a lot of listening through media monitoring and research in the belief that the first thing we had to do in communication was to understand the problem.

The notes said: At MB, we have come to recognize very clearly that we operate only by public consent. That is true of every business and the challenge is to retain public consent to operate our business. We realize at MB (then Canada's largest forest products company) that we are entrusted with the management of a natural resource owned by the people and, since we operate only by public consent, we have a responsibility, a duty, to report on our stewardship. The public has a right to know. We have an obligation to communicate.

We have to do a good job in our business – and we have to communicate so that the public knows we are doing a good job. We have to earn credibility and public trust – first, by proper performance of our business, by carrying out our responsibilities as a corporate enterprise, and second, by communication which brings public knowledge and understanding of that performance.

If we are to succeed in growing as a financially viable institution while making a contribution to the community in its broadest sense, the prerequisite is credibility. And we will never achieve credibility unless our communications are accurate reflections of corporate integrity. The most clever manipulations of public opinion will not conceal for long the true nature of an organization whose integrity is compromised. Business and industry today are under constant public scrutiny that will strip away every effort to create a cosmetic image. What the public sees must be the real thing, warts and all.

That basic philosophy underlies our communications efforts. We try to be positive and candid in what we have to say, whether we say it through executive statements and speeches, news releases, interviews, corporate publications or through paid platforms.

Even in 2019 – against all of the controversy surrounding Donald Trump's approach to media and communication – I believe such a basic philosophy makes huge sense for any business or other institution that wants to earn credibility and retain public consent for its existence. Similarly, I believe the philosophy that drove MB's "ideas" or "corporate" advertising approach at that time, remains sound. MB used paid time and space to communicate company policies and philosophies and to promote the company's name as distinct from product advertising.

The presentation notes continued:

Why should business and industry do such advertising at all? The position taken at MB for a dozen years was reflected by a statement made a year or so ago by Rawleigh Warner Jr., the Chairman of Mobil Oil Corporation which adopted corporate "idea" advertising about five years after MB began using the concept. Mr. Warner said: " . . . if we hadn't done it, we would have left all the media to our critics. Somebody had to answer, and that's what we tried to do."

Generally speaking, MB fared pretty well with the news media, was treated fairly in day to day coverage in the news columns and newscasts – on the whole. But MB couldn't – and didn't – expect the media to think that everything it had to say, that its policies and philosophies and all its good deeds were newsworthy. We knew that our warts would be newsworthy, of course, and that our critics didn't – and still don't — have too much difficulty in getting heard through news space. The news media was usually generous, as well, in carrying MB's response. But that, in our view, was not enough to meet our duty to report our stewardship.

So we used paid space — to describe our policies, philosophies and practices. We strove to do so in a timely manner which anticipated public concerns and provided clear, factual information from which public understanding would develop.

The starting point for our success in this communication was to assess accurately the climate of public attitudes so that our communications – and our performance – could be guided by management informed of public concerns and desires. Such research was done regularly to test or reinforce our own observation of the changing scene and the results were taken into account in preparations for corporate advertising.

The presentation notes made these points:

". . . Our corporate campaigns have done much to establish a national presence for MB and, as a well-known corporate name, we have been able to make strong and useful national statements on such issues as tax reform, trade policy, bank act revisions and capital requirements of the forest industry.

We benefit in other ways, too, from corporate campaigns. Marketing personnel report that national exposure given the company on television provides them with instant recognition when they call on customers. Our reputation for sponsoring programs of exceptional quality helps establish our credentials with educators. A national presence, plus the accounting we give of our role in the forests, makes us better understood in the investment community and it helps in our recruitment of employees.

MB's success in Television at the time came largely because its commercials were prepared with great attention to assure the material was factual, informative and, above all, interesting. It was based on the belief that the public deserved a full accounting of performance and that we should not bore the public to death in the process.

MB's corporate advertising at that time included newspaper and magazine inserts describing the company and its involvement in the forests of British Columbia, its home base. Four were titled "A Walk in the Forest" "The living Forest" "Enjoying the Forest" and "How the Forest Grows"—all of them containing facts about the forest resource and MB's stewardship of it. TV commercials were mini-documentaries on operating techniques, new methods used in forestry and manufacturing in the industry, as well as about the company's sponsorship of such community projects as MB Place at the Van Dusen Botanical Gardens in Vancouver, described earlier, and its sponsorship of Tommy Tompkins and his wildlife films.

MB was selective in its use of television, finding and sponsoring high-quality programs that attracted different mixes of age groups and interests. Post-show audience analysis each time told us the show involved had drawn to our corporate messages a large audience of educated, articulate viewers, many of whom were opinion leaders in their own spheres of activity.

In Canadian TV, MB was the first sponsor to base its commercial breaks on the content of the sponsored program rather than on the clock. We chose shows of 90 minutes or more in length so we could get appropriate weight for our messages while arranging our commercial breaks so as not to intrude on the dramatic flow of the production. MB scheduled on the assumption that much of the value of the message is lost if insensitive commercial breaks caused public irritation.

Someone once described the MB commercials as visual essays – interesting, factual and entertaining. The combination of sponsoring quality shows, scheduling commercial breaks judiciously and producing factual and interesting material paid real dividends. People remembered MB TV spots for their messages rather than for the number of times they saw them.

> A viewer in Nova Scotia wrote to MB: "... I found that the movie was complimented by your advertising which did not insult my intelligence or sense of logic by portraying a childish skit and continual redundancy ... "

> A viewer in Quebec wrote: ... Your TV commercials came across strongly to the point one hardly realized he was watching a commercial. Having been in the advertising business for some 40 years, I had a special interest in your style of messages."

And from Ontario: ". . . It is refreshing to see a company that produces intelligent and informative advertisements especially when dealing with one of Canada's rapidly diminishing major natural resources. This in itself is a major accomplishment but you have exceeded my expectations by not only your interest in the environment but also the fragile relationship between the environment and wildlife. Your obvious concern with this delicate symbiosis is to be highly commended."

Two more Ontario viewers wrote: " My daughter, age 12, is now more interested in the way lumber companies such as yours not only cut trees and put them to so many uses, but that you even take time to replant the forest. It is one side we never think you fellows ever consider but are always told of the mass destruction some companies leave in the forest."

"It was the first time in my experience that I looked forward to the next commercial. They were informative and so expertly executed."

And one from Campbell River, B.C. said "It is high praise indeed when I tell you I had to take time out from the play to pour myself a drink because I did not want to miss any of the commercials."

Over a decade, hundreds more comments stood as testimony to the benefits of choice of quality shows and quality fact-based commercials. The MB commercials ran 90 to 120 seconds in length. No slogans were used in them. MB abhorred slogans and it tried to state its corporate case quietly. Each subject was researched by its own staff, written for TV use by the best talent MB could find, inside or outside the company, and produced by the best film makers the company could find, film makers who worked directly with the company. Those commercIals demonstrated that MB cared about the forests it managed, that it was aware of human values and was concerned with the quality of life in communities where it operated.

Our print specials – 12 pages for newspaper inserts, 8 for national magazines including Time and Maclean's – followed the same principles as the TV commercials and brought similar successes – with content based on facts, creatively presented. Use of scientific facts which even teachers found they could rely on to augment school texts and use of good photography and art work produced specifically for the purpose made these publications popular.

In my five years with MacMillan Bloedel, it became apparent that employees enjoyed this approach to communication as much as many in the public audience and the understanding they encouraged helped employees stay focused on doing the good job that gave credibility to the company and its communications.

Imagine if such attention to performance was encouraged by fact-based communication about an energy company's work with Aboriginal communities to ensure everyone shares appropriately in the benefits from the resource's development. Relationships could become far more positive; there would be less opportunity for extremist environmentalists and other anti-development protesters to use Aboriginal groups to their advantage; pipelines might even get built. Such are the lessons I believe the MB experience of way back then can deliver to today's corporate advertisers, whether they're using traditional or social media that didn't exist in 1977.

I also believe there are valuable lessons for current energy developments in two major energy-related clients we served through the MacFarlane Morris Peacock agency. Those came after my sojourn as a member and then Director of the Public Affairs Department at BC Tel.

## 31

## FROM AGENCY TO DIRECT BC TEL EMPLOYEE AND BACK AGAIN

When I joined the Public Affairs Department of BC Tel in November 1977, Gordon MacFarlane was the company President and CEO and Colin Patterson was Public Affairs Director. His predecessor, Jim MacInnes, had become Vice-President of Marketing. My posting was as Communications Projects Manager.

I was located in the then new BC Tel building nicknamed "The Boot" on the Burnaby side of Boundary Road at Kingsway Avenue which became the executive office location just before I started my employment there. I worked with many BC Tel departments on documents for filing with regulators, provincial government departments and agencies and shared writer-in-residence duties for my first year or so with Bill McAfee, a talented writer who prepared speaking notes for the CEO and others in the company.

When Colin Patterson was posted to new responsibilities, I was appointed Director of Public Affairs, reporting to Barry McNeil, Vice-President Finance and Administration. That brought the family another automobile, a black Chevrolet sedan that was part of the BC Tel fleet. It came with its own parking space in The Boot's garage and was a perk I found hard to give up.

In that role, I had responsibility for a department that carried out employee communications programs, media relations, advertising and promotion, provided research abilities and a corporate library.

Many people I had met and worked with during my O'Brien days now reported to me: Bryan Holiday as ad manager, Keith Matthews as employee communication manager, Freydis Welland as a writer-researcher and frequent advisor on strategies. Ken Metheral, who once had been my boss as a CP Bureau Chief, was editing an employee newsletter.

My executive assistant who helped me keep up with all of the bureaucratic paper work required in a corporate environment, was Valerie Simons, who I met along with husband Robert when they were attending B.C. Institute of Technology and actively engaged as leaders in Young Variety while I was Variety Club's Chief Barker.

The Simons became residents of Port Moody and Jean and I saw them frequently at local functions where we were all involved as volunteers. Robert became President of the Port Moody Foundation, among other things, and ran, unsuccessfully, for Mayor on one occasion. Valerie was chosen as president of the Port Moody Arts Society and still held the post as we entered 2019.

My resignation from BC Tel was effective February 29, 1980, having advised McNeil that I was planning to join the MacFarlane Morris Public Relations agency to prove to myself that I could survive in the competitive world of business as an owner-participant.

At a going-away function held at my departure, I received a coin telephone, an engraved likeness of The Boot, and several other mementos including a small book into which hand-written notes from people throughout the company were pasted. One, signed simply Gordon, came from the CEO, Gordon MacFarlane who wrote: "Jim, here's hoping the MacFarlane you're joining appreciates you as much as the MacFarlane you're leaving. Best of luck."

On March 1, 1980, I became a Vice-President and owner-partner in MacFarlane, Morris Peacock Ltd. George MacFarlane had started the agency in 1969 after serving as the Vancouver correspondent for The Toronto Globe & Mail newspaper and a short stint in public relations work with the Lovick agency. He continued as President and senior partner, focusing much of his time and energy on Jack Poole and the Daon Development Company led by Poole.

Jack Morris, a colleague from days we both worked for The Canadian Press, was executive Vice-President; Darlene Young was a Vice-President working closely with George on the Daon activities, where she exhibited outstanding creative abilities in organizing attention-generating grand openings for Daon's 999 West Hastings building in Vancouver and for Park Place on Burrard between Georgia and Dunsmuir, adjacent to Christ Church Cathedral.

Among other agency staff then were Linda Persiani, Christine Lindstrom and Nancy Pitre. Nancy was a single mom whose son, Jamie, handled three assignments for our agency – inside mascot costumes. Thanks to Jamie and Nancy I'm able to recall some detail here: In a Hallowe'en promotion at B.C. Place, Jamie was Peter Pumpkin. In a Variety Club promotion at SCIENCE WORLD he was Sonic the hedgehog, and he was Mr. Turtle in a chocolate promotion. Jamie remembers teaching then Vancouver Police Chief and Variety Club President Bob Stewart and his wife Barbara how to play some video games but when he met them again at his wedding to Linda Stewart – a niece of Bob's – he had to remind them they'd met when he was Sonic, to which Bob remarked "OMG was that you?"

Our agency's offices were located on the Sixth Avenue side of the Pacific Press Building on Granville Street, home to The Sun and The Province which had moved from The Sun Tower and

JIM PEACOCK

The Province building in which I spent my CP working days. By then, the two papers were owned by Pacific Press. Our tenancy in the building gave us access to the Pacific Press Cafeteria where many discussions took place with reporters and editors. And the building was across Granville Street from the Vancouver Press Club quarters, where more of the same often occurred after normal work hours.

When 999 West Hastings opened, we had a small suite of offices there for a time – on the same floor as an eventual client named Ridley Terminals which built a coal port in Prince Rupert to ship coal from northeast B.C. mines at Tumbler Ridge. The Executive Assistant to the Ridley Terminals CEO was Kim Ross whose brother Brian founded Third Wave Communications, a video production business.

Later, when our agency outgrew its space at 999 West Hastings, we moved to an earlier-built Daon building at 1040 West Pender. Third Wave became a tenant in our offices there and when an opportunity arose we introduced Brian and his largely family crew to a client at the University of B.C. seeking video production help. Third Wave did an excellent job – and its business just grew after that.

Morgan: Newsletters and Publishing Limited, owned and operated by Peter Morgan, also became a resident in our offices – and proved to be a great resource in producing newsletters for many of our clients, including McDonald's, Building Safety Week, Montenay, the Western LNG and Hat Creek projects, to mention a few.

In due course, Terry McDowell moved into our office space and conducted an advertising business that included promotion of golf course developments in Richmond, the Okanagan and on Vancouver Island. Terry also became a director of our company. And soon after that, when Peter Downes retired from MB, Peter also joined our Board and provided counsel and assistance on client recruitment until his death at age 75.

## 32

# NAMING SCIENCE WORLD AND HELPING TO FUND ITS DEVELOPMENT

Helen Patterson was the wife of Colin, who was my first immediate boss during the time I spent as a part of the BC Tel Public Affairs Department. She also was very active in political circles and in public relations roles on behalf the B.C. Business Council and the $3 billion North East Coal development that saw major new coal mines opened in the Tumbler Ridge region.

Our agency did some work for her on Northeast Coal and with her when we acted for Ridley Terminals, the Prince Rupert coal terminal through which output from Tumbler Ridge was shipped to Asian markets. Through her political involvement, she was well acquainted with Barbara Brink, whose lawyer husband Russell was a mover and shaker in the Federal Liberal Party. Barbara became the driving force behind bringing Vancouver its SCIENCE WORLD attraction following Expo 86.

From early days watching her own sons respond to interactive displays at science centres in Ontario and elsewhere, Barbara had an interest in such hands-on educational facilities. In 1977, having been asked by the Junior League of Greater Vancouver to research a major project for Vancouver that would benefit children and add to the quality of life in the city, she joined forces with the city's social planning department. They began discussing the possibility of a science centre.

The first step was to form the Arts Sciences and Technology Centre Science World Society and then to join a planning session with science centre directors from other cities. In a magazine published to mark the 1989 opening of SCIENCE WORLD BRITISH COLUMBIA, Barbara recalled: "We were a bunch of well-meaning people, but we didn't have a clue when it came to programming or administration."

The visiting directors approved of a plan to combine arts and sciences, saying this would make a Vancouver science centre unique in North America. In a 1980 test of public response 55,000 people attended *Extended I*, a program of 80 exhibits staged at the Vancouver Planetarium.

Subsequent evidence of interest resulted from an outreach program that took exhibits to communities around the province and in January 1982 Block Brothers Industries offered the Society the use of a building at 600 Granville Street for a demonstration centre. With Barbara Brink as society president and Junior League leader, the Arts, Sciences and Technology Centre operated there from 1982 to 1988. In those six years it drew more than 600,000 visitors and served another 400,000 through outreach programs.

When Expo 86 came to Vancouver, Brink was determined to find a permanent facility to deliver so much more than could ever be expected of the demonstration centre. She was determined to bring a world class facility to Vancouver and saw the potential to achieve that employing an Expo 86 structure after the world exposition ended in October, 1986.

She set out with her AS&TC Board of Directors to plot a drive to make it happen, including a substantial public fund-raising program. She spearheaded the campaign that obtained the Expo Centre to house this dream, secured $12 million from all levels of government and the balance from the private sector and individuals to meet the ultimate $19.1 million retrofit and exhibit costs to

*Remember the Good Times*

create Science World British Columbia for its May 6, 1989 opening.

As she prepared for the campaign to get the Expo Centre and the capital to convert it, Barbara recognized that a short, punchy name would be needed for marketing. On Helen Patterson's recommendation, Barbara sought advice from our public relations firm. As the account executive, I was advised that the AS&TC Board members had rejected several name suggestions because they insisted the facility should not be simply science or technology, but needed to encompass the arts.

After a discussion with colleague Julie Marcus, I proposed "Science World" and, to assist in convincing the Board to accept it, had illustrator Gil Dyer put the words SCIENCE WORLD beside the AS&TC logo and above an underline reading: "The Arts, Sciences & Technology Centre." The Board gave its unanimous approval to:

**SCIENCE WORLD**
**The Arts, Sciences & Technology Centre**

In due course, to reflect the province-wide importance of this Expo 86 legacy, the name became SCIENCE WORLD BRITISH COLUMBIA. The underline that helped to bring the AS&TC Board's approval was no longer necessary. In 1988, Barbara announced the new logo: The name: SCIENCE WORLD British Columbia. The Logo: a stylized version of the Expo Centre, a geodesic dome built at the edge of False Creek at the Quebec Street entrance to the Expo 86 site.

The name came from our shop. The logo concept and design were by Karen Hadden, Chris Gould and Darwin Lee, senior creative staff of Vrlak, Robinson Hayhurst Communications under direction of Brian Follet. The finished artwork was by Karo Design Resources.

Our agency also prepared a marketing strategy and plan for a fund-raising campaign, including

JIM PEACOCK

the name change. I was assigned to work as public relations advisory committee chair, with Barbara Brink, President of the AS&TC Science World Society; J. Haig deB. Farris, who chaired the fund-raising committee; his vice-chairs, John Pitts and Milton Wong; campaign director Wendy Bradley; for a time Carol Tulk, Associate Director; Norman Fletcher (when he was hired Oct. 1, 1987, as Managing Director with responsibility to build the place) and 15 other committee members, among them many senior executives from technology, forestry and other companies in B.C.

As this is written in 2019, the wonderful facility that resulted is marking three decades of successful operation and has been given the name Science World at Telus World of Science, in recognition of a major financial contribution by Telus to the ongoing costs of maintaining Science World.

The geodesic globe – or, "The Ball" as it became popularly known through a campaign slogan "Keep the Ball Rolling" – had a royal endorsement from Queen Elizabeth II and Prince Philip, with a little help from then Vancouver Mayor Gordon Campbell. The Royal Couple were on a visit to the city and Mayor Campbell was given the opportunity to choose an activity for their participation on a given day. He chose a visit to the Expo Centre on October 15, 1987, in company with Federal government ministers Pat Carney and Frank Oberle, and British Columbia's Premier William Vander Zalm and Stan Hagen.

Nearly 30 staff and volunteers, along with 300 school children put on a special SCIENCE WORLD show prepared for the visit, Then Queen Elizabeth II dedicated the Expo Centre as "SCIENCE WORLD. A science centre for the people of British Columbia".

Against that background, those promoting the fund-raising

efforts to make this dream come true went to work – and by September 11, 1987, an announcement was made that three levels of government had committed $11 million towards the costs. The sum included matching grants of $5 million each from the Federal and B.C. governments and $1 million from the City of Vancouver. The Greater Vancouver Regional District later added $1 million to bring the government total to $12 million.

The capital campaign that generated $7.1 million from the private sector really got going in 1988 with a kickoff dinner in April, featuring Cecil Green. Green was a brilliant young University of B.C. scientist who left Vancouver in 1923 to attend Boston's Massachusetts Institute of Technology (MIT) and went on to co-found Texas Instruments in Dallas in 1930. TI's 1987 revenues were $5.59 billion.

Haig Farris convinced Green to lend his name and support to the SCIENCE WORLD campaign and with that kind of support many corporations, foundations and individuals responded. The BC Tel Group, the W.J. Van Dusen Foundation and Imperial Oil were among the first major donors. B.C. Hydro, Fletcher Challenge Canada, Mr. & Mrs. W. Maurice Young, Fei and Milton Wong, Haig and Mary Farris – the list of donors included virtually every company of any size in British Columbia, ranging from Alcan to Westinghouse and included MacFarlane Peacock Ltd.

By May 6, 1989, when SCIENCE WORLD was officially opened, a public appeal had been added to the campaign and it successfully filled the remaining $2 million gap to bring private sector totals to $7.1 million. The refurbished building had 10,200 square metres of space with dozens of hands-on exhibits in five new galleries and the largest OMNIMAX dome screen in the world. During its first year of operation, it welcomed 705,000 visitors and visited 96 B.C. communities with its outreach programs.

In a letter dated June 13, 1989, Haig Farris wrote: "Dear Jim, On behalf of SCIENCE WORLD, I would like to express my deep appreciation for all your hard work and creative ideas. Your good sense and imagination had a lot to do with our success. I hope it gives you great satisfaction to see thousands of visitors streaming into SCIENCE WORLD."

In a letter dated July 25, 1989, Barbara Brink wrote; "Dear Jim: With two and a half months behind us since we opened, and 200,000 visitors later, I wanted to take this opportunity to thank you on behalf of the Board of Governors for all your hard work on behalf of SCIENCE WORLD. A tremendous amount has been accomplished in a very short period of time and your hard work, enthusiasm and energy were crucial to our success. Together we can all be proud of our contribution to Vancouver and British Columbia. Over the years to come you can look proudly at what you began – you will always know that you were part of the team that "Got the Ball Rolling".

Two other special events for me followed as a result of my involvement with SCIENCE WORLD and Barbara Brink. They involved visits to Vancouver by Benazir Bhutto, former president of Pakistan, on January 22, 1991 and by Mikhail Gorbachev, former president of the USSR, on March 27, 1993.

Bhutto spoke to the first World Affairs Dinner, presented by the Junior League of Greater Vancouver and SCIENCE WORLD, and having been in the news frequently before arriving in Vancouver, was in demand by the news media. A news conference was scheduled. Daughter Peggi was working with our agency at the time and she and I handled media relations, publicity for the event and the news conference with President Bhutto.

Her Excellency was a treat to work with, so very professional, and when she had responded to the last question she had time to deal with, she turned to Peggi and me and asked if that was enough. We closed if off with ease, she thanked us and departed to prepare for her dinner speech.

> "Thank you for an outstanding job once again," Barbara Brink wrote later. "You and Peggi handled all the details so well, it was one area that I knew that I need not worry about. Thank you for

getting the stories to the media and arranging the interviews and the press conference. . . I am sure the entourage that accompanied Her Excellency were impressed with how well the day went."

The Gorbachev Dinner was presented by SCIENCE WORLD alone. His visit included the dinner and time at SCIENCE WORLD where he met a number of young students and was photographed blowing on a large soap bubble during a science lesson from a staff member. SCIENCE WORLD held a contest to choose 10 students to meet Gorbachev and attend the dinner. Claire de Lisser, a Grade 11 student from Queen Elizabeth High School in Surrey, was one of the 10 and had her story and photo published in the Surrey/North Delta Leader March 28, 1993. "This is a great opportunity to meet someone who's done so much. It's an opportunity you can't pass up."

Rita Creurer and I handled media relations for both the SCIENCE WORLD visit and the dinner and subsequently received this note from event coordinator Jackie Shrive:

"Many, many thanks for all you did to ensure the success of the Mikhail Gorbachev visit to Vancouver. You did a superb job of keeping the media informed and we got wonderful coverage for SCIENCE WORLD, probably the best we have ever had! You are great to work with."

## 33
# ENERGY DEVELOPMENT AND ABORIGINAL RELATIONS

I was assigned the lead role in serving Dome Petroleum Limited of Calgary, at the time a successful petroleum company pursuing huge projects, some of them identified as possible developments along British Columbia's Pacific coast. Dome sent Vice-President Andy Younger to Vancouver in search of communications help related to several possibilities for resource development on the West Coast. A petro-chemical plant was one consideration. A plant from which to ship liquefied natural gas (LNG) was another. The company had purchased an industrial property at Britannia Beach, south of Squamish and beside the entrance to a closed copper mine that became a mining museum.

In the first months of our agency's Dome assignment, the focus was on Britannia Beach. A community developed there during the years of the mine's operation, providing residences for mine employees. After the mine closed, some employees who now lived in Squamish claimed a sort of squatters rights to several cottages along the Howe Sound waterfront, between the railway tracks and the beach. They used them as summer vacation spots, spending time in and around them enjoying homemade wine (harsh and potent, red in large Coke bottles, white in large 7-Up or Ginger Ale bottles) and as overnight camp out sites.

For Dome to develop any project at this property it first had to convince those using these sites as free summer cabins to vacate. Part of the process saw me meet with small groups and then some individuals who understandably were reluctant to go. On a couple of those occasions, I was invited to share in the homemade wines. That sharing was limited because I had some driving to do when the meetings were over – but I sampled enough to be able to make the "harsh and potent" judgments mentioned above.

Eventually, Dome made financial settlements with all concerned and with minimal protesting the beach area was vacated. Later, Dome disposed of the holdings because the anticipated chemical plant was abandoned for business and environmental reasons.

Dome continued its search for a site to build a terminal to ship LNG to Japan – and when the project managers homed in on Grassy Point, across the bay from Port Simpson, the major work began for me as the agency's account executive serving Dome and its project partners.

It was a 2½-year assignment that took me to Calgary many times, to Prince Rupert even more often – and on several occasions in company with agency staff member Laurel Redman who assisted in running a Prince Rupert information office. I flew on a corporate jet flight with a group of Port Simpson's Lax Kw'alaam Band Council representatives to Kenai, Alaska to visit an operating LNG facility and to Ottawa and Victoria to participate with project and Lax Kw'alaam Council members in meetings with government authorities.

The project approach was successful; an agreement was signed with the Band, no voice of opposition was raised at National Energy Board hearings held in Prince Rupert, Indigenous leaders praised project management and the Band for their foresight in negotiating a mutually-beneficial agreement before going to the NEB. Economic conditions changed; energy prices fell, Dome entered bankruptcy and the Western LNG Project died.

On January 5, 1986, I prepared this commentary on the Western LNG project for the Legal Services Society Schools Program Newsletter:

> In the debate surrounding native Indian land claims, two things ought to be clear by now: First, settlement of land claims will take time. Second, the issue is impairing industrial development in British Columbia, particularly in the natural resource industries.
>
> The latter should be unnecessary – but not everyone agrees on how the province's industrial development can move ahead smoothly while aboriginal claims are resolved. British Columbia can find one recent and excellent lesson in this regard in the experience of the participants in the Western LNG (Liquified Natural Gas) Project.

THIS PROJECT INVOLVED PROPOSED investment of approximately $4 billion to transport surplus Canadian natural gas to Japan through pipeline, liquefaction and deepsea shipping facilities. Its principal proponent from the start was Dome Petroleum Limited of Calgary, in partnership with the Japanese trading company, Nissho Iwai Corporation. The Indian Band involved is the Lax Kw'alaams of Port Simpson, a coastal village on Tsimpsean Indian Reserve land 30 kilometres north of Prince Rupert.

Several other companies became involved in the project over the nearly six years from its 1980 start until it was abandoned in 1985 because of declines in the world economy and especially in energy demand and prices. Dome is the only one mentioned here because Dome led the project in building a relationship with the Lax Kw'alaams Band.

Dome and the Band found a successful process through which the Band was able to support the LNG project without being concerned that its position on land claims was being impaired. The process was founded on goodwill, understanding, consideration of the other's point of view, effective communication and patience. Together, these allowed a sense of trust to develop between the two – and upon that trust, they built a legal agreement which worked to the advantage of both.

Many individuals played a part in the achievement. Principal among them from Dome were Dr. A.H. Younger and Jerry van der Linden, P.Eng. On the Band's side were all members of the Council, and particularly James Bryant, Albert White and Robert Sankey, staff member Bill Ostenstad and lawyer Harry Slade.

A full history is not possible here. In summary, Dome examined 26 B.C. coastal sites as potential locations for the $2 billion liquefaction plant and ship-loading terminal. As Port Simpson Bay became the leading candidate, Dome was advised by its public relations counsel (MacFarlane Morris Peacock of Vancouver) that it should act directly to acquaint the Port Simpson people with the idea and get their response.

Dr. Younger, then a Dome Vice-President and leader of the LNG project, acted on the advice immediately. With the help of several people, including individuals in the Federal and B.C. governments, a meeting was arranged. Four representatives of the project met in Port Simpson with members of the Band Council.

Many meetings followed – involving the Band Council, its specially-appointed resource development committee, the community as a whole and a wide range of representatives of the project. The Band wanted to act responsibly, to make decisions based on social, economic and environmental information generated for it, to protect the fishery and the environment in the area, and to obtain the greatest possible Band participation in the project's economic benefits.

With no financial resources of its own to devote to these tasks, the Band requested – and received – funding from Dome and had social, economic, public safety and environmental studies done. Dome agreed to the funding after long and hard negotiation, taking into account the potential cost of project delay if public protest or court action resulted. In this decision, and in the subsequent agreement between Dome and the Band, the project managers also recognized that the village of Port Simpson did not have the ability to collect municipal taxes from the project and thus had to find other ways to share in its economic benefits.

On October 14, 1983 – 2 ½ years after the first Dome-Band meeting, the two signed a formal agreement setting out condition for the development. The agreement acknowledged the existence of the Band's aboriginal claim. The Band agreed it would not use that claim as grounds to oppose the project.

James Bryant, Chief Councillor during much of the negotiating period, described the agreement as nothing short of "history making for my people of Lax Kw'alaams." Indian and Northern Affairs Canada, in a special issue of "Afffairs" said. ". . .it seems clear that, if success is measured by the extent to which people decide their futures, the agreement is an important achievement for the Band."

*Chief James Bryant and Dr. Andy Younger signed agreement*

The agreement was filed in evidence during the National Energy Board hearings into the project's application for licences. It was in no small way responsible for the fact that the public hearings in Prince Rupert, for which the NEB had scheduled seven sitting days, required only two days of sittings. Others in the native Indian community of northwestern B.C. commended both sides for their foresight.

There is much more to this experience, of course. But this much perhaps will indicate that there is a process for successful pursuit of economic development while aboriginal claims are resolved. The process requires people of goodwill and the patience to develop relationships to the point of trust.

In the course of this work, I became acquainted with the long-time mayor of Prince Rupert, Peter Lester. He visited Vancouver for a variety of reasons and on one of those visits we ended up in the same restaurant at dinner—Umberto's. I was there with the Dome project manager, Jerry van der Linden, who Mayor Lester knew from meetings in his city. Next time I met the mayor, he expressed surprise that he'd find the head of the Dome project dining with his public relations counsel.

Some time after the Western LNG Project came to an end, a proposal to construct an oil pipeline from Alberta to Kitimat was the focus of some debate. I entered the discussion with this October 9, 2012 letter to The Vancouver Sun:

**"Re: Energy Advocate doubts Enbridge will follow through**

Richard Neufeld is right on the money in supporting a pipeline to carry Alberta oilsands products to a Pacific Coast port to provide access to Asian and other markets. He's correct, too, in his claim that Enbridge is not likely to be accepted in B.C. as the entity to do it. On July 16, 2012, I sent that same message to Enbridge and to my MP, the Hon. James Moore. I wrote the following:

'I firmly believe that Enbridge has so sullied its nest that it will never get approval to build this project across B.C. I also believe that your government puts its support in our province, if not elsewhere in Canada, at enormous risk if it continues to show unbridled support for Enbridge in this project.'

"I based those thoughts on experience living in B.C. for more than 50 years and being involved for 30 years in the Public Relations field. One of my clients some years ago was Calgary-based Dome Petroleum, which, in partnership with a Japanese trading company, planned a multi-billion-dollar project to ship natural gas to Japan through a Liquefied Natural Gas plant located at Port Simpson.

"After 2 ½ years of carefully planned and executed relationship building, this project went to a Prince Rupert hearing by the NEB, which set aside two full weeks for the purpose. In 2 ½ days, the hearing ended, having heard praise from the Lax Kw'alaams Indian Band and from Miles Richardson, then leader of the Haida, and having had not a single objector before it. This in the wake of an original-announcement headline in the Prince Rupert News that read: "Floating H Bomb" above a photo of an LNG ship. That project came to an end when the energy market prices collapsed to the point where it was no longer economically viable - but it had earned respect and public support.

"In light of all of the developments surrounding the Gateway project, including the scolding of Enbridge over a spill in the U.S., I believe a new proponent should be found to take this project out of the hands of Enbridge, then build the kinds of community relationships that instill public confidence in both the project proponent and the regulatory process. From my reading of the reaction of broad segments of the public in British Columbia, Enbridge has virtually no hope of having its proposal accepted in British Columbia, no matter the outcome of current hearings.

I am long-since retired and probably won't still be around when final decisions are made on this development proposal. But for the good of all those who will be, I sincerely believe a whole new approach is essential. My opinion, for sure, and perhaps not worthy of note. But I hope it might be a useful insight from one with 50-plus years of understanding of what makes the Pacific Coast province tick."

As it turned out, I was still around when the Federal government killed the Northern Gateway project. On November 29, 2016 Prime Minister Justin Trudeau ordered the NEB to dismiss the Enbridge application.

## 34

# ANOTHER ENERGY PROJECT – HAT CREEK

For many years B.C. Hydro eyed the huge resources of the Hat Creek valley, described in the January, 1982 issue of Energy magazine as "a sweet dream for engineers, a nightmare for environmentalists". The Hat Creek Valley, 200 kilometres northeast of Vancouver between Cache Creek-Ashcroft and Lillooet, contains steam coal deposits estimated at 10 to 15 billion tonnes. In the early 1980s B.C. Hydro, which had studied these deposits since 1957, assembled a special team under the leadership of Maurice Favel, P.Eng. who was assigned as Hat Creek Project Manager, to prepare for a possible development application.

Our agency won an assignment to assist the project with communications, including media and community relations activities. The Fact Sheet we prepared described the project as a coal-fired thermal plant to burn steam coal from an open-pit mine to generate electricity to meet projected needs in British Columbia. Had it proceeded, it would have been the first thermal plant in the province, which until then relied on hydro-electricity generated by water power from dams on many of B.C.'s rivers.

The project team was conducting work to define the coal

resource and to address environmental and economic requirements in preparation for a licensing process that was expected to start in 1983. If approved by all of the necessary regulatory bodies, construction was intended to begin in 1985 to have first power produced in late 1990. The cost was projected at more than $5 billion. Some $10 million was invested in the preparation of an Environmental Impact Statement which would have been subjected to public scrutiny in hearings by the B.C. Utilities Commission. Before construction could start, with a project work force of 3,000 at its peak, the project needed a B.C. Energy Project Certificate indicating it could meet requirements established by government agencies under several pieces of legislation.

While Maurice Favel and his team – which for a time included our eldest daughter Virginia in her capacity as an Industrial First Aid attendant at the Hat Creek site – were working on all of the economic, environmental and technical elements, Pam Bottomley an employee of our agency, and I were operating a project information office in Vancouver and another in Cache Creek. We helped the project respond to media inquiries, worked to inform community groups and First Nations and to keep project team members apprised of developments. I had met Pam earlier when she was married to Rick Hyde, a member of the BC Tel Public Affairs department. She eventually married a BC Hydro employee and moved to Vancouver Island.

As an aside, Virginia's role at the project site prompted my wife to set out on another of her travel adventures, this time boarding a train in North Vancouver to ride alone past Lillooet into the open spaces of the Hat Creek Valley and there, with no railway station within many kilometres, be pick up and taken to camp for a visit.

The two basic objectives of our Hat Creek Project communications plans were: One, to communicate to the widest possible audience accurate information about the project; and Two, to listen to public response and identify concerns so that appropriate action could be taken to respond to those concerns. With

*Remember the Good Times*

full support from Favel, his team and B.C. Hydro, we operated on an open and frank basis, providing public access to project information as it developed, actively seeking ways and means to increase public knowledge of the project and the studies made and being made into its potential impacts, and actively participating in community discussion of the project.

In the first two months of 1982, with excellent support from the project team, status reports were delivered to the elected councils of the villages of Ashcroft, Cache Creek, Clinton and Lillooet, the City of Kamloops and the Thompson-Nicola Regional District. Presentations were made to B.C. Hydro employees in 100 Mile House, Williams Lake, Peace Canyon and Hydro's Gordon Shrum generating station. Briefings were provided to the Progressive Conservative federal caucus; service clubs in Kamloops and Hope, and the annual meeting of the B.C. Institute of Agrologists.

We were able to cite some positive outcomes from such communication. A letter to B.A. (Tony) Angel, a senior member of Favel's staff, followed his presentation to Ashcroft Council. Mayor Ward L. Bishop wrote: "Once again, our thanks to you for your very informative visit to Council on February 8, 1982. Your comments regarding ten-year hydro demand projections were very clear. It is unfortunate that more people do not fully comprehend the significance of our economy on projects of such magnitude as the Hat Creek one. Your communication with Ashcroft continues to be excellent."

The Vancouver Sun of February 22, 1982 carried a report by Shelley Banks in which she quoted a local rancher named Gordon Parke, a staunch opponent of the project up to the time he attended the Institute of Agrologists discussion. Parke told that meeting he had "suffered a few amendments" in his views on the project since Hydro first announced it. "From outright rejection, I find my opinions tempered a bit by information from B.C. Hydro and independent observers." In an interview, Parke told Banks "It's stupid to oppose it if it's just me that's bothered by it. I won't oppose it unless I'm convinced there are larger reasons."

In the end, B.C. Hydro, at the time headed by CEO Robert Bonner, a former B.C. Attorney General in the Social Credit government of W.A.C. Bennett and one of the politicians I had covered while with CP, decided to postpone the Hat Creek Thermal project indefinitely.

When the decision was taken to shut down the project at the end of August 1982, Maurice sent me a letter that included these comments:

> "I would like to take this opportunity to thank you and Pam Bottomley for your innovative and effective provision of public affairs and information services for the project. Rest assured that the decision to postpone the project does not reflect any shortcomings in the public communications programme you developed, in fact quite the opposite.
>
> "In my view the present public perception of the project has become much more informed and potentially acceptable, notwithstanding the scare-monger tactics of the media and organized minority opposition groups. Bearing in mind the prototype nature for B.C. residents of a coal-fired thermal project and the importation of the acid rain issue from the East, I feel the relative success of the project's communications programme vis a vis other more conventional projects merits commendation."

In my response to those comments, I acknowledged that communications can only reflect the foresight and understanding of the project leadership and its employees. I wrote:

> "It is unfortunate that conditions have led to the decision to postpone the project indefinitely after so many fine people put so much effort into preparing for it. Your kind comments about the work Pam Bottomley and I have been able to do as part of the Hat Creek Project Team are very much appreciated by both of us.

We're rather proud of the accomplishments of the last two years, not so much for what we may have done ourselves but for the way you and others involved with the project have made it possible to be effective in the information and community relations areas.

"It has been a privilege and a pleasure to work with you, particularly because you have demonstrated such sensitivity to and understanding of the need to communicate, both with employees and with the public."

## 35

# CHIEF COMMISSIONER CONNAGHAN READ THE OMENS ACCURATELY

Charles J. (Chuck) Connaghan was appointed the first Chief Commissioner of the British Columbia Treaty Commission on April 15, 1993. I was assigned by our agency to prepare a communications plan and work on its implementation. The initial media fact sheet prepared described the Treaty Commission as a unique, independent and impartial body established by the governments of Canada and British Columbia and the First Nations Summit, representing the majority of First Nations in B.C. The Commission's role was described as being to manage a voluntary, made-in-B.C. process to facilitate the negotiation of treaties in B.C.

The Commission was appointed in accordance with an agreement signed on Sept. 21, 1992 by members of the First Nations Summit, Prime Minister Brian Mulroney and Premier Michael Harcourt. The agreement endorsed the 1990 British Columbia Claims Task Force Report which recommended the new treaty negotiation process for B.C.

The Chief Commissioner was jointly appointed by the Summit, the Federal Government and the Provincial Government. Two of the Commissioners were appointed by the Summit and one by each of the Federal and B.C. governments.

Chuck Connaghan, who earned his BA in 1959 and Master of Arts in 1960 from the University of B.C., had served as the founding chair of the B.C. Roundtable on the Environment and the Economy, was a former president of Construction Labour Relations Association and former Vice-President, Administration, University of B.C.

One Summit-appointed Commissioner was Carole T. Corcoran, a UBC Law graduate (1990), a Dene, born and raised in Fort Nelson, who had worked with Band and Tribal Councils and served as a Commissioner with the Federal Indian Claims Commission. The other was Douglas C. Kelly, a Sto:lo from Soowahlie, near Chilliwack and Manager of Operations for the Sto:lo Tribal Council.

Lawyer Barbara L. Fisher was the B.C. government appointee. The Federal appointee was Dr. Lorne Greenaway, a veterinary surgeon who had served as Member of Parliament for Cariboo-Chilcotin.

I learned a lot about aboriginal issues in British Columbia through my work in assisting the Commission with media communication, preparation of speaking notes for the Chief Commissioner and content for the Commission's annual report. These notes from a speech Connaghan gave to the Simon Fraser University's President's dinner on February 16, 1995, provide a summary of the challenge the Commission was still trying to solve in 2018:

> ". . . In 1763. . . King George III issued a royal proclamation which recognized Aboriginal title and, in essence, directed that lands and resources should be acquired from Aboriginal peoples only by the Crown and only by treaty. The spirit of that proclamation appears to have been accepted by successive Canadian governments since the 1850s. By that time the British Crown had entered into treaties with First Nations in Eastern

Canada. And, as European settlers moved westward treaties were concluded with First Nations across the Prairies.

"West of the Rockies, the policy stalled, with the exception of the Douglas Treaties, entered into by James Douglas, the Hudson's Bay Company's Chief Factor who later became the second governor of the colony of Vancouver Island. These 14 treaties covered less than 400 square miles of the island.

"The B.C. Mainland became a colony in 1858 and London continued to direct Douglas to enter into treaties. But no more were arranged. Instead, First Nations were offered the same opportunity as afforded settlers – the Aboriginal community could acquire Crown land and become farmers. Few did because it ignored their wishes, their culture and Aboriginal title.

"The non-Aboriginal community of the day assumed that First Nations would abandon their cultural heritage, become farmers, and become a part of the non-Aboriginal community. Several reserves were established for First Nations people. No compensation was offered to First Nations for the loss of traditional land and resources.

"In 1871, when British Columbia entered Confederation, the majority of the province's population were First Nations peoples. Yet the First Nations were not included in the decision-making. The terms of union gave control to the Province for the creation of further Indian Reserves. Canada assumed responsibility for First Nations people and the reservations. Continued exclusion from their traditional lands and resources forced the First Nations people to rely on federal support programs. That led to their current level of dependency.

"They did not take this treatment without objection. During the late 1800s, they outlined their demands to Aboriginal title and recognition of rights. But they seldom used direct action until 1898, when Aboriginals established a protest blockade near Fort St. John that halted access to the Yukon by miners attracted by a gold strike. The Federal government solved that problem by extending Treaty Eight from what now is Southern Alberta into the Peace River area of British Columbia. B.C. entered the 20$^{th}$ century with only 15 treaties covering a small portion of B.C. land with a very small number of the province's nearly 200 First Nations Bands. That is still the situation today. . . . "

Chief Commissioner Connaghan also told that audience:

"I am convinced that treaty-making through voluntary negotiation is the best way to settle Aboriginal claims. The courts told us that many of the matters brought before them should be negotiated. The alternatives will be costly court cases, disruptive civil disobedience, as was becoming obvious in 1990, and the destruction of hope for a people who had been convinced that government were at last committed to addressing their long-standing concerns. B.C. Treaty-making is about more than land and money. It is about new relationships. It is about bringing a significant segment of the British Columbia's population into the economic and social mainstream of our province. It is about showing respect for a people, their traditions and their culture. It is about treating them as full citizens of our community, not as wards of the state."

Many events in British Columbia since those comments were made have proven how accurately Chuck Connaghan read the omens of the Province's future. Both demonstrations and court decisions came to the fore especially in 2018. They totally disrupted plans for a multi-billion-dollar expansion of the Trans-Mountain Pipeline to bring increased amounts of petroleum from Alberta to the Pacific Coast, creating huge financial, environmental and social consequences across Canada.

*Remember the Good Times*

Chuck Connaghan did not survive to see his predictions come true. On October 26, 2003, while he, his wife Erma and his long-time close friend Jack Bibby were preparing to leave a Gulf Islands retreat, Connaghan, who was just 61 years old, literally dropped dead. Bibby told me that one minute Chuck was standing beside him and a heart-beat later had crashed to the floor.

## 36

## FIVE MCDONALD'S AT EXPO 86 – A FOUR MONTH ASSIGNMENT THAT LASTED 17 YEARS

Early in 1986, as Vancouver prepared for a world exposition — Expo 86 – I was in the right place at the right time to become the account executive assigned to McDonald's Restaurants of Canada Limited. The company came seeking public relations assistance to deal with controversy that erupted when it announced its intention to operate a floating restaurant on the False Creek site following the fair. The floating restaurant – nicknamed "McBarge" — was one of five outlets McDonald's operated on the Expo site throughout the six-month event.

The controversy was stirred by some members of Vancouver's City Council, notably outspoken left-winger Harry Rankin, who were taken by surprise. McDonald's had dealt with Expo 86 authorities and the provincial government – but not the City of Vancouver — in putting together its Expo 86 arrangements. Our agency had a working relationship with Palmer Jarvis Advertising, McDonald's ad agency, headed by Frank Palmer and George Jarvis. Palmer came to the MacFarlane Morris Peacock offices with Ron Marcoux and several of his management team.

JIM PEACOCK

*McDonald's Floating restaurant, Expo 86*

I was a recent addition to the agency, was available to handle new business, and I knew Ron from some mutual involvement with the Variety Club of Western Canada. When he and his team decided to hire us for the job, expected to last four months, I got the up-front assignment. Seventeen years later, Ron had retired and I closed out Peacock Public Relations Ltd. and the assignment ended.

What a ride it was. Initially, we were able to generate a lot of positive news coverage because McDonald's decided its five Expo 86 site restaurants, including the unique floater built on a barge on the shore of False Creek, would charge the same prices as its off-site outlets.

We arranged an interview for Ron Marcoux with the Business Editor of The Province and it resulted in a highly positive section-front photo and story. Later, with George Cohon, the President and CEO of McDonald's Canada, and a team of McDonald's franchisees and managers from across Canada in Vancouver for a convention that coincided with McDonald's Day at Expo, we had

*Remember the Good Times*

a hand in getting the new B.C. Premier, Bill Vander Zalm, on stage.

And when the Premier announced there that the Provincial Government would match funds being raised by Rick Hansen, who was wheeling across Canada in the final leg of his round-the-world Man In Motion wheelchair epic, I recorded what he said, transcribed it and got it to the news desk of The Vancouver Sun, which ran a small but important item on its front page. The coverage reinforced the connection between McDonald's and the Man-in-Motion project. Ron Marcoux helped Rick Hansen launch his tour, telling Rick that he (Ron) thought he (Rick) was crazy to take on such a huge challenge but if he insisted on wheeling around the world to focus attention on and raise funds to support those confined to wheelchairs and related mobility aids, McDonald's would put up $25,000 to help get him started. Rick Hansen displayed the McDonald's logo throughout the tour.

In a letter dated Sept. 17, 1986, as Expo 86 was nearing its conclusion, Ron Marcoux provided an assessment of the success of our assignment with McDonald's Canada, Western Region. He wrote:

*Dear Jim:*

*As you probably know, one of the decisions I had to make was to change my original opinion of what an outside public relations firm could do for McDonald's. I was always of the opinion that a good, home grown, down-to-earth, opened dialogue communication with the media by myself, or others that have worked and built this Company to what it is today, was the best public relations we could get. I still believe it unless you can bring on the services of someone as competent as yourself and your firm. I guess what I'm saying, Jim, is that I have changed my mind due to the benefits I think are evidenced in the kind of press that we are getting now, and the kind of results through the media that weren't there before. All the result of one James Peacock. Thank you Jim for changing my mind and for all the effort you have put into our account. It's been a big plus having you as part of our team.*

JIM PEACOCK

*Arnie Nelson Award winners l to r Al McLeod, Jim Peacock, Frank Palmer with Diane Nelson, Jack Pettitt and Ron Marcoux*

Another indication of the satisfaction with our performance came later when, as President of Peacock Public Relations, the successor to MacFarlane Morris Peacock, I became the first recipient of the 1995 – and first — Arnie Nelson Achievement Award. Some logistic problems delayed the presentation until Dec. 14, 1996 at the Region's annual Christmas dinner celebration. There Ron Marcoux presented the award and its $3,000 in McDonald's Corporation common shares to Jean and me. The accompanying letter reads: "In the eyes of the selection committee, you have demonstrated the attributes associated with the Arnie Nelson Achievement Award and made a significant contribution to the Company and its goals."

The award was created to honor Arnie Nelson, a part-time member of the Crew of the first McDonald's in Canada, opened in 1967 on No. 3 Road, Richmond. Nelson rose through the ranks to Senior Vice-President for the Western Region. He died of a heart attack in November 1964 while at work. He was 42. I had worked very closely with Arnie on any number of communications projects and was quite involved in putting together a news

*Remember the Good Times*

announcement of his sudden passing and notes for use in ceremonies at a celebration of his life. He and his wife Diane were dedicated workout participants and had the muscles to prove it, which made Arnie's death that much more shocking to most who knew him. Diane was involved in coaching hockey and running hockey schools and in the subsequent years I helped her with related communications.

Promoting McDonald's people and events, including McDonald's Day, throughout Expo 86 kept me busy. McDonald's already had an off-site restaurant on Main Street, just a block away from the site of the geodesic Expo Centre that later became Science World. When Annette Willoughby rose through the ranks to become manager of that outlet, we were able to generate news coverage of her role and of McDonald's promotion of females. Annette later became a Human Resources Consultant, working with Human Resources Manager Ken Bathurst, like me a former MacMillan Bloedel employee.

The five McDonald's outlets on the Expo site set records for sales and patronage and their success made news across the McDonald's system. It all created opportunities for more media exposure and Ron Marcoux became a regular guest on some of Vancouver's most watched and listened to TV and radio open line shows, among them Rafe Mair on CKNW and Jack Webster on BCTV.

On August 15, 1986 McDonald's officially recognized the company's growth to 500 restaurants by designating the company's first floating facility in Canada as the "Friendship 500". And, as part of that dedication, McDonald's committed to raise throughout its system of restaurants $250,000 for Rick Hansen's Man-in-Motion World Tour. In fact, McDonald's Canada and its franchise partners raised $1.5 million.

The fact sheet prepared for the ensuing opening of a new Western Canada headquarters building added that McDonald's helped make it possible for Hansen to take his campaign on a

JIM PEACOCK

25,000-mile route through 34 countries, touching five continents. Feeding crew members and offering facilities to assist in fund raising activities, McDonald's owner-operators world-wide provided additional support for this tour.

## 37

# A POST-EXPO TRIP DOWN UNDER

The six months of Expo 86 kept our agency busy with several clients in addition to McDonald's. Telecom Canada, whose pavilion chief was Jim MacInnes of BC Tel, also claimed much of my time in media promotion of its Disney Circle-Vision 360 degree film "Portraits of Canada" "Images du Canada" featuring sites, sounds and people of Canada filmed in communities across the country, including Igoolik, Northwest Territories, on the Arctic Ocean, home of Beluga whales. Peter (Tatigat) Arnatsiaq was in a scene with his dog team and Peter Kipsigak was shown with his snowmobile.

That has relevance to one of my happy Telecom Canada Pavilion tasks because, in recognition of their participation in the filming, several high school students were brought from the Arctic region to Vancouver to visit Expo 86. In their remote northern community, they watched a CBC TV show filmed at the Vancouver Public Aquarium, which at that time housed two or three Beluga whales from the region. I escorted the group on a visit to the Aquarium where they were thrilled to see the site of the TV show and, for the first time in their lives, to see live Belugas. Parents of one or two of the students hunted Belugas in the Arctic but these students hadn't reached the age where they got out on the ocean waters that were home to Belugas.

*This group of students from Igoolik were brought by Telecom Canada to Expo 86, where Jim escorted them on a visit to Vancouver Aquarium.*

In any event, when all of the Expo excitement and agency work there was completed, Jean and I packed up for some travel—to Perth, Australia with stops in Fiji and New Zealand and a visit to Brisbane on the way to Perth. Brisbane was preparing for the next world exposition – Expo 88 – and I toured their site and talked to organizers so I could report to media back home.

On our return, I sent notes to Beryl Wilson, who edited a small community newsletter serving the False Creek area of Vancouver.

I told her about the progress in preparation for Expo 88, then added this:

"I would like to tell you a little bit about a small piece of paradise visited enroute to see the Aussie wonderland. It's called MALOLO LAILAI and is one of hundreds of islands in Fiji. The hand-painted sign adjacent to the grass and gravel landing strip says: 'Plantation – Customs, Immigration – Muskets, Frowns, Swords, Shoes, Spears & Worries prohibited.' And so they are, though no policeman is needed to enforce the prohibitions.

"The reference to weapons has its seeds in history. The local recollections are that the first overseas owner of the property acquired it in exchange for two muskets, which the aboriginals found more effective than swords or spears. The fact that the bay between Lalolo and Malolo Lailai Islands is called Musket Cove gives credence to the story. Most everyone encountered at Plantation Island Resort seemed to take seriously the ban on frowns and worries – but some shoes were in evidence, especially at mid-day when the sun was hot.

"Malolo Lailai (Lailai means little) has no streets and no vehicular traffic, save for a couple of lailai tractors and their wagons, used to transport luggage, passengers and resort supplies. If you vacationed on the Hawaiian Island of Maui a decade or two ago, the peace and quiet of Plantation Island Resort and its neighbor, Dick's Place, will have enormous appeal. The sunshine is hot. The sandy beaches are long and uncrowded. The South Pacific waters are warm and beautiful. The pace is easy, relaxed. The resort staff, most of them Fijian, are attentive but unhurried. The architecture of the accommodations fits with the landscape – nothing is more than two storeys high and most buildings have thatched roofs.

"There's a delicate blend of Fijian and European cultures.

Similarly, you can sample local dishes or enjoy typical European or North American meals. Among the guests, you'll find a predominance of Australian accents, with a few New Zealanders thrown in to confuse you. Visitors come in numbers, too, from the United States, Canada and Europe. The Plantation Island Resort, with 40 spacious rooms in a two-story hotel complex, 45 thatched-roof bures and two dormitories – can accommodate up to 350 people and even when filled the resort's 23-acre site isn't crowded.

"Malolo Lailai is just 10 minutes by air – in a Sunflower Airlines twin-engined 10-passenger British aircraft appropriately named "'the Islander' – from Nadi airport on the main island, Viti Levu, where inernational flights arrive. Many visitors reach the resort by boat aboard the catamaran ferry Island Express, which cruises daily from Nadi Bay.

"Breakfast, lunch and dinner are served in the resort's open-walled dining hall, which also houses a lounge where Fijian and other entertainment is provided nightly. The 'Love Feast', with traditional Fijian dishes, including pork and beef cooked all day in barbeque pits, was followed by a concert of Fijian music and dance, performed by resort staff, several of whom then surrounded the 'kava' bowl with its chocolate-colored milky liquid produced from pepper roots."

After our stop at Plantation Island, we flew to Auckland, New Zealand to spend a few days exploring sheep farms and watching the shearing process, to go through the Waitomo caves with ceilings covered with the lights of glowworms, and Maori Museums, complete with works of art and live entertainment by Maori singers and dancers. We travelled to Rotorua and Te Whakarewa Valley to see the Pohutu geyser, mud pools, hot springs, silica formations, the Kiwi birds and to visit the national schools of wood carving, weaving, stone and bone carving. These treasures have been shared with manuhini (visitors) for 170 years.

From Auckland, it was off to Brisbane, Australia. We found Brisbane, Australia's third largest city at the time with 1.3 million population, to be bustling. Work on the 40-hectare Expo 88 site across the Brisbane River from the downtown core was ahead of schedule in site preparation and pavilion construction. The fair's theme was Leisure in a World of Technology and it ran from April 30 to October 31 in 1988. I had toured the site and talked with organizers. Then, Jean and I took a boat excursion on the Brisbane River to get a close-up look at bats hanging from trees along the river banks, ugly but fascinating creatures.

Our flight from Brisbane to Perth made a stop at Alice Springs, where Jean and I disembarked for 20 minutes. Leaving the air-conditioned aircraft felt like walking into an oven – 40 degrees celcius – but it was fascinating to us to see many Aussie residents wearing broad-brimmed hats with tiny balls hanging at the end of short strings all the way around the brim. With a shake of the head, these balls shooed away black flies. We saw Ayres Rock from our plane's windows, along with vast open space.

Our purpose in travelling to Perth was to attend Pacrim 86, an international conference on trade and finance and investment opportunities in the Asia-Pacific region. Business in Vancouver had promoted the conference and travel packages in partnership with the Aussie Pavilion at Expo 86.

Participants included Bob Hawke, then Australia's Prime Minister, and by video President Ronald Reagan of the U.S. The conference coincided with the 1986 America's Cup yacht races on the Indian Ocean out of Freemantle. One convention event was a cruise aboard a luxury catamaran that we shared with about 300 other passengers. Sparkling wine flowed accompanied by fine food and, since it was a practice day for the yachts, many of them sailed past our craft, some at a speed which made it difficult to get a still photo without a blur.

Our agency in Vancouver had a working relationship with a

Toronto group that had the Canada II yacht as a client. As a result, we were able to visit the Canada II enclosure in Freemantle to watch as sails were measured, trimmed and sewn after being stretched by the winds during a day of practice. Amazing process, with sewing machines, long shallow trench-like facilities built to accommodate the huge, tall sails, plus computers for measurement accuracy.

## 38

# MCDONALD'S ASSIGNMENT RESUMED

The McDonald's assignment resumed once our Australian travel ended. It included helping McDonald's take advantage of many opportunities for media promotions based on newsworthy happenings. McDonald's Canada celebrated its 20$^{th}$ anniversary on June 1, 1987. That made news. So did the official opening of a new $10 million Western Canada headquarters building on Still Creek Drive in Burnaby, on July 28, 1987, by which time the number of outlets in Canada had grown to 525.

On that occasion, then Economic Development Minister Grace McCarthy of the B.C. government told the gathering: "It is a pleasure to celebrate such a magnificent addition to our province, knowing that it is entirely the result of entrepreneurial spirit for which both McDonald's and British Columbia are famous." The acting mayor of the City of Burnaby, Vic Stusiak, congratulated the company for the style and esthetics of the glass and metal structure and for choosing to keep its Western region administrative headquarters in his municipality. George Cohon, president and CEO, McDonald's Canada, and Marcoux said the new facility reflects McDonald's past and anticipated future growth in the West.

To mark the event, Ron presented a cheque for $11,000 to Gordon Winter, chair of the Burnaby General Hospital Board, to pay for a pediatric fetal heart monitor for use in labour and delivery rooms where 1,500 babies are delivered each year.

The Fact Sheet for that event described the building as a contemporary, free-form glass and metal structure two-storeys high, designed with an atrium as its heart. It has a solarium perimeter to ensure a bright and airy atmosphere throughout its wall-less second-level office area. The main level contains training rooms with current technology for effective teaching and training, employee fitness centre, employee lounge, meeting rooms and storage facilities, all in the area surrounding the atrium. General access to the office level is by open stairways from the raised area of the atrium floor. An elevator provides wheelchair access.

Owned by McDonald's Restaurants of Canada and occupied by the administrative and training staff of the company's Western region, the building also serves as the Western campus of the Canadian Institute of Hamburgerology, where training is provided for 600 to 700 employees each year. It initially was home for about 75 employees, with room for expansion in its 3,000 square metres of floor space.

My work included preparing plans and materials for use in media, employee and public communication, much of it related to such events as those described above but also to many individual happenings carried out by franchisees frequently in partnership with company community relations staff to promote coverage of community participation – everything from fundraising for local causes to encouraging fire-safety education.

Plan To Get Out Alive arose from an idea brought to McDonald's attention in 1984 by an Edmonton fire fighter named Tim Vandenbrink. He had observed the success of fire drills in schools, drills from which children learned how to get out safely if a fire should occur. Ron Marcoux looked at the idea and said let's give it a try. The program was introduced in Edmonton in 1990 and soon became a major promotional part of Fire Prevention Week in Western Canada and then nationally and across the United States. Ronald McDonald often was a part of these activities because of the way children responded to him.

Much of my time was devoted, as well, to promotions related to Ronald McDonald House programs and fundraising, including McHappy Day held annually since 1977 to raise money for children's charities. Ronald McDonald Houses provide a home away from home for family members who have to bring children to these locations for cancer or other hospital treatment. The first Ronald McDonald House in Canada was opened in 1981 in Toronto. Houses followed in Vancouver (opened October 4, 1983) and then in Edmonton, Calgary, Saskatoon, Winnipeg, London, Ottawa, Montreal, Quebec City and Halifax. A second was opened later in Toronto and the original Vancouver House was replaced in 2014 by one providing 73 bedrooms, adjacent to B.C.'s Children's Hospital.

In 1984, McDonald's established RMCC – Ronald McDonald Children's Charities of Canada –a non-profit foundation which has donated many millions of dollars to Ronald Houses and other children's charities over the years. RMCC is largely funded by McHappy Day, a regular unique-to-McDonald's event when celebrities, politicians, municipal officials, show business personalities, sports figures and neighbors join the people of McDonald's to help serve Big Macs and other products. From each Big Mac or other designated product sold, McDonald's contributes $1 to children's charities. The program started in 1977 and the first six annual McHappy Days generated more than $6 million for the purpose. Millions more have come in the ensuing 35 years.

Each McHappy Day while I served McDonald's, I worked with Ron Marcoux and Palmer Jarvis on media visits to encourage public participation, accompanying Ron to locations from which media were broadcasting live. At day's end we

JIM PEACOCK

would advise media of the day's outcome, generally more than $1 million across Canada.

When McDonald's celebrated its 20th anniversary in Canada in 1987, one off my projects was a newsletter that described 20 years of growth from one outlet to 525 across the country, including 162 in the West, 76 of them in British Columbia. It also focused on the importance of employee training, McDonald's support for regional suppliers of products and services in the food, packaging and delivery services that keep the restaurants going, and on the changing styles of buildings housing their outlets. And it outlined many ways in which McDonald's and its licencees support their communities, including hamburgers for schools and Orange Bowls to help in fund-raising for school projects, Good Sport Cards for amateur sports teams and Golden Arches Cards giving seniors a benefit.

In partnership with Peter Legge's Canada Wide Magazines Ltd. McDonald's marked its 25th anniversary, publishing a 50-page magazine distributed by B.C. Business magazine setting out the company's history, economic impacts, operating philosophies, product development, including pizza introduced in 1991, and a profile of Ron Marcoux.

The latter reminded readers that Marcoux fought long and hard to get McDonald's into Expo 86 where five outlets were located on the site, including the Friendship 500, McDonald's first floating restaurant in Canada. These restaurants had the highest sales volumes in the world at the time. "We ended up selling a dollar's worth of hamburgers for every man, woman and child going through the turnstiles at Expo," Marcoux said – 20,000,000.

The article went on to report that winning his Expo battle with head office took a monumental amount of effort and persistence for which Marcoux was awarded the prestigious Press On Award, presented in memory of McDonald's founder Ray Kroc. It is the highest in-house award you can get. The inscription reads: "Nothing in the world takes the place of persistence. Talent will not; nothing is more common than unsuccessful men with talent.

Genius will not; unrewarded genius is almost a proverb. Education alone will not; the world is full of educated derelicts. Persistence and determination alone are omnipotent."

"Persistence is a better word than stubborn," says Marcoux, who would go on to receive in 1994 both the "Marketer of the Year" recognition from the Sales and Marketing Executives of Vancouver, and the Golden Heart Community Achievement Award from the Variety Club of British Columbia. At the dinner where he received the Golden Heart Award, Grace McCarthy, a member of the Social Credit Government cabinet, told the audience a couple of little-known stories about Ron's community service.

In 1990, when the Greater Vancouver Regional District undertook a planning project called "Choosing Our Future", Ron came to the table to sponsor a student poster program that injected into the considerations the views of some 700 students. And, McCarthy said, "Ron didn't just say, okay, here's the money. He spent a Saturday with four others judging the artwork and announcing the names of those who'd been judged to have made the best contributions for their grade level. And he spent another Saturday morning not only hosting but attending a breakfast for those students. That's community commitment."

McCarthy also recalled that some seven years earlier, *a young lady from Richmond named Katie Luxton was in need of a heart transplant. Those weren't being done in B.C. at the time so the family turned to the leading heart transplant centre in North America, Pittsburgh's Children's Hospital. The Luxtons needed help. Ron came to the table – not only to bring along McDonald's in B.C. but McDonald's and Ronald McDonald House in Pittsburgh, where the family stayed during the transplant surgery and recovery period.*

In 1987, after Katie's successful transplant, Ron wished Katie and her family every success during a small party at the new McDonald's headquarters building. Katie was the guest of honour and, in typical fashion, Ron treated her with the warmth and kindness of a gentle grandfather. Katie had a great time and, at the Variety function, McCarthy said: "Ron, I know you will be interested to hear this: Today, Katie is a healthy teenager, competing in school sports, chasing boys and doing everything a normal teenager does."

Ron also won recognition for his service to and support for Special Olympics, including serving as Honorary Chair of the Canadian and Provincial Special Olympics Games. And he served as Honorary Patron, in bringing to the Lower Mainland of B.C. the innovative Giant Steps program for children with severe learning disorders. Motivation for his persistence in that area was a grandson with autism.

In the midst of the work, I was invited to join Ron Marcoux and Vice-President Jack Pettit for lunch at the Hart House restaurant in the Burnaby neighborhood near where McDonald's first Western Region headquarters was located. The two of them presented me with a very special Bulova wrist watch, the face of it depicting in a gold-colored engraving of a McDonald's restaurant with a Golden Arches logo sign. It is a treasured reminder of the good times I enjoyed with this client. It still keeps perfect time in 2019 and has become a conversation starter several times at my retirement residence.

# 39

# MORE ACCOLADES FOR RON MARCOUX
## MANY ACTIVITIES SHARED WITH ARTIST BARB WOOD

Ron Marcoux's volunteer activities brought him another accolade, in 1993: In April of that year I sent notes to City Scene items Columnist Joy Metcalfe about Volunteer Vancouver's 50$^{th}$ anniversary dinner at the Waterfront Centre Hotel where 50 individuals and organizations were saluted for what Mayor Gordon Campbell of Vancouver, as Master of Ceremonies, described as their contribution to the quality of life in this city.

Ron was among those saluted, he for a long list of volunteer involvements described elsewhere in more detail. So was then Lieutenant Governor David Lamb, who like all of the other recipients of the honor received a limited edition copy of a Barb Wood etching done especially for Volunteer Vancouver. It was one of the many occasions I had to encounter Barb over the years until her untimely death from a heart attack March 19, 2014 at the too young age of 61.

Significant McDonald's projects in which Barb and I participated included the April 10, 1991 Ronald McDonald Children's Charities (RMCC) Ski Challenge at Whistler, a major fund-raiser, and a 30$^{th}$ anniversary poster.

For the Ski Challenge, Barb prepared a unique work of art that focused on the Chateau Whistler, where the event's reception and dinner were staged. It contained sketches of many of the event's leaders and participants. The drawing had space front and centre for one more image – that of the buyer which Barb added after the auction that helped boost the proceeds. Barb did an updated version of this artwork for the menu cover for the RMCC Ski Challenge of April 16, 1993.

Barb also prepared art work for posters used in promoting Plan to Get Out Alive and other community programs and, as McDonald's approached the 30th anniversary of the opening of its first restaurant in Canada, she was commissioned to do a special work. Its sketches featured Ronald McDonald as if completing a painting of the first restaurant – a take-out-only structure located on No. 3 Road in Richmond, B.C. and opened on June 1, 1967. The poster contained 27 smaller images depicting everything from McHappy Day lapel pins, Ronald McDonald Houses, restaurants, office structures in Toronto, Quebec and Burnaby to Rick Hansen, Expo 86, Special Olympics and the Plan to Get Out Alive fire prevention program. All of this above the caption reading: Serving Canadians for 30 Years.

In April 1991, when I was helping the Council of Canadian Building Officials promote "Building Safety Week" messages, Barb put together a poster featuring a Pig appearing through the window of a red brick house and holding building permits to grab attention for the headings "Building Safety is No Accident" "Build Safe. Build Smart. Get your permits before you start!"

For the Youth Forum of November, 1991 – to which Grace McArthy referred in her Variety Club comments, Barb prepared a special poster to invite young people to "Put yourself in the picture" through submissions to the B.C. Round Table on the Environment and the Economy.

Barb Wood became a good friend to both me and Jean, who spent time with Barb at events like the RMCC Ski Challenges, and who often joined me when I met Barb at lunch or in her studio on Granville Street in Vancouver. They often shared stories about their growing children – Ginny, Kerry and Peggi on Jean's side, Arthur and Roger on Barb's, and had hearty laughs at some of the episodes they described.

Jean was a party to the decision to purchase the original of Barb's hand-coloured etching titled "Really Pleasant Morning at Pleasantside, Port Moody", a whimsical drawing of the Pleasantside Grocery on Ioco Road, just above Old Orchard Park. In 1995, Barb had a show that was a tribute to historic corner stores in Greater Vancouver. Pleasantside Grocery was one of 36 of her works related to stores she referred to as "a place of bread, milk and gossip and a centre for neighborhood notices."

She said at the time: "The old corner stores are important to me. They're places of rare and disappearing architecture, many of them original landmarks in charming old wooden homes where the storekeepers and their families lived upstairs." The article describing her tribute said: "Among the far-flung places Wood loves is Pleasantside Grocery ("out in Port Moody, a real landmark").

When a gallery that sold some of Barb's art closed, a framed and hand-coloured copy of the original we purchased became available. Jean was a major user of the Port Moody Public Library until vision problems forced her to turn to audio books. She and I purchased the special copy from Barb in 2007 and donated it, in company with the artist, to the Port Moody Library, where Barb helped to unveil it and where in 2018 it was hanging in the main reading area as a reminder of some of Port Moody's past.

I had one other memorable project with Barb Wood – she prepared cover artwork for the 1991 Capital Campaign conducted by the B.C. Cancer Agency under the leadership of Barbara Brink, the moving force behind the drive that brought SCIENCE WORLD BRITISH COLUMBIA to life. Barbara Brink invited me to work with her on the communications elements of the campaign, which had been started under different leadership and was failing. Literature prepared for the original campaign kickoff was drab and more likely to cause depression than to inspire gifts. Barb Wood's whimsical approach to a very serious issue changed that. She sketched a small aircraft towing a banner. The banner read: B.C. Cancer Agency Capital Fund Campaign and led the eye to lettering on the airplane's wings that said "Spirit of Hope". A positive start.

The campaign set out to raise $5 million to purchase new equipment and to improve existing facilities – tools which Brink described as essential to continued success in beating a disease which touches everyone's life and directly affects one in three British Columbians.

An image of the B.C. Cancer Agency building near Vancouver General Hospital was depicted in Barb Wood's artwork and it included various notes: "You can help" "make a pledge" "Thanks" "Oh Boy New" "Re Search" "Patient Care" "Goal: Several Million $" "Equipment".

The text, pamphlets and other supporting literature were equally positive. The campaign succeeded and the agency acquired the needed equipment and facility improvements that included a library, two new patient waiting rooms, eight laboratories and Bone Marrow Transplant Radiotherapy Facility Special Oncology Ward used for bone-marrow transplant patients.

## 40

# WASN'T THAT A PARTY!

### IT PRECEDED THE FORMAL CLOSING OF PEACOCK PUBLIC RELATIONS

On October 15, 1991, Bob Williamson convinced me that we had a late-day meeting with a potential client at the B.C. Club on the Expo 86 site. The locale had served as The Canadian Club during Expo 86 and our agency had retained access when it was converted to a new private club use. When Bob and I entered it on this day we were greeted by a room filled with family, friends, clients, media, agency members and colleagues assembled secretly to salute my $60^{th}$ birthday that came two days later on the $17^{th}$. A huge surprise!

My photo album from the wonderful event – in which Jean and our daughters Peggi, Kerry and Virginia played a major organizing roll – shows pictures of Jack Poole (Daon) and wife Darlene; Ron Marcoux, Arnie Nelson & Jack Pettitt (McDonald's), Frank Palmer and Brenda Granlund (Palmer Jarvis Advertising); Brian Holliday, Peter Harvey, Freydis Welland (BCTel) and her husband Mike Welland; Ray Lord, Jackie Shrive and Wendy Bradley (SCIENCE WORLD); Barb Wood (Barb Wood Graphics) and husband Don Hazeldon; Art Jones (founder of what now is Global TV); Peter Forward (Canadian Facts) and his wife Marcie; Bob McKenzie (Marine Printers) and wife Verity; Allan Sinclair

JIM PEACOCK

(Council of Forest Industries) and his wife Ruth; Barbara Stewart (Variety Club), Dan Howe (Special Olympics), Peter Morgan (Morgan News), Brian Ross (Third Wave), Terry McDowell (McDowell & Associates).

*Darlene and Jack Poole flank Jim*

Family members included Jean, Peggi, Kerry and then husband Eric Vandersanden; Virginia and Lance Balcom; my brother Jack Peacock, his wife Bunny and their daughter Nola with her then husband Rob Vandersanden, niece Karen and her husband Wayne Baldock, and the parents of Rob and Eric, Nick and Alice Boons.

Friends and colleagues included Nancy Pitre and son Jamie, Dolly and Ben Kopelow, Jack and Janet Enefer, David and Diana Finlay, Dennis and Sonia McLennan, Dan and Carolyn McArdle, Lynne & Don Monk, Jack and June Elliott, Eunice Nicoll, Del & Hal McLennan, Lori Janson-Haig, Mike Cvitkovich, Russell Dale, Laurette Leduc, Trudy Sandland, Annette Berry, J.J. Richards, Bob Weins, Sally and Ian Street.

The event was advertised as a roast and, while I don't recall too much of the banter by those who spoke, Joy Metcalfe reported in her North Shore News column of Oct. 27, 1991 that guests included (thanks to Palmer and Marcoux) "Marilyn Munroe" in her Seven Year Itch dress, "crooning the sexiest Happy Birthday tune that Jim had ever heard!"

By the time that party took place, the make-up of the agency's partnership had begun to change. Jack Morris resigned as Executive Vice-President and secretary May 5, 1987 and moved on to focus on real estate investing.

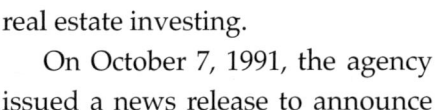

*Marilyn, Jack Pettitt, Jim and Ron Marcoux*

On October 7, 1991, the agency issued a news release to announce that its chairman and founder George MacFarlane had sold his interest in the company to Jim Peacock and Bob Williamson. The release said Peacock, who joined the company in 1980 and became its president in 1989, became chief executive officer. Wiliamson, who had 10 years with the company by then, was executive vice-president. The agency's board of directors continued to include Terry McDowell and Peter Downes. Both resigned as directors January 31, 1992.

A few days earlier, on January 27, 1992, Marketing magazine published this announcement:

PR OWNER PEACOCK TAKES PEACOCK ON ITS OWN

VANCOUVER – Jim Peacock has become the sole owner of MacFarlane Peacock Public Relations and changed the name to Peacock Public Relations. MacFarlane Peacock was founded in 1969 by former Globe and Mail Vancouver bureau chief George MacFarlane. Peacock has also established a working relationship with the Freelance Group, headed by ex-Anderson Advertising president Phil Cunliffe. With the new partnership, PPR intends to offer a variety of marketing advertising and public relations services.

By the end of March 1992, I had become the sole proprietor of PPR. I moved the company's offices along with two employees – Nancy Pitre and Rita Cruerer — first into a house on Ontario Street in Vancouver owned by Brian Ross and occupied by Third Wave Communications. As circumstances changed and most of my contact with clients was taking place at the clients' locations, I moved the office home, working out settlements with Nancy and Rita.

My daily commute amounted to a walk downstairs to the recreation room at 902 Garrow Drive, Port Moody where I had desk, board room table, massive photocopier and computers. The business was formally closed in 2004 after Jean and I had moved to our NewPort Village condo.

*Darlene Poole, George MacFarlane and Jim at a November 2018 luncheon celebration in Nanaimo of George's 94th birthday, a highlight of a long and interesting chapter for all three.*

## 41

# RON MARCOUX RETIRED AFTER 30 YEARS

The end of the Ron Marcoux era at McDonald's in Western Canada came in 1998. The closing chapter began May 7 with internal distribution of a letter Ron wrote to employees, licensees and suppliers in which he said:

"As you have no doubt heard, I will be retiring from McDonald's at the end of the year. The decision to do so has been partly mine, with a little nudge from the Canadian Board of Directors – but after a good deal of thought, I think it is the right decision. As most of you know, I love the work I do and the people involved in all areas of the Company. Perhaps over the years my commitment has resulted to some extent in the exclusion of a private or personal life - but I have no complaints. Everyone who receives this note can take a lot of pride in knowing that together we have built our Western Canadian Company into one of the most respected in McDonaldland. Thank you for that place in history."

In the news release sent out to make this decision public, Ron was quoted:

"I've had a great time for three decades with McDonald's. It has been very rewarding to be surrounded by so many talented, creative, hard-working and fun-loving people within the company in Western Canada, among our franchisees across the west and with our many suppliers. It has also been a privilege to be a part of a company that is so involved with the community and the volunteer organizations who contribute so much. I still have several interesting months of work ahead, but I'm looking forward to 1999 when I'll have more time to pursue a number of community service activities that have become very personal and close to me, particularly in the area of autism."

Marcoux, 66 at that time, was president of Giant Steps of Greater Vancouver Developmental Society, then seeking to open a Giant Steps centre in the Lower Mainland to help children and families cope with autism. He also led Skate For Hope, a foundation established to help fund the Giant Steps program in B.C. (In fact, a Giant Steps Centre was opened in Coquitlam and it operated for about a year, serving Ron's grandson, among many others, before running out of funds.)

Ron served McDonald's until December 31, 1998, when he wrote to the McFamily again to say:

"The year 1998 has come and gone and for me – just like the last 30 years – in what seems like the blink of an eye. During that time, together we have built a very successful and very respected Canadian company – a Company to which we have all been contributors and for which we are deserving of the good feelings that come with a successful effort.

We did it by paying attention to the basics and keeping it simple. Ray Kroc was the best keep-it-simple, customer-side marketer who ever touched me. I've said it many, many times, but it's appropriate to repeat it here – he was the best. I learned, and tried to pass on to everyone in our organization, Ray's basics of Q.S.C.& V. (Quality, Service, Cleanliness and Value) which could be bottom-lined as customer satisfaction. Ray used to emphasize that everything that happens before McDonald's meets the customer is all for naught if the customer experience isn't totally satisfactory. . . . . Thanks for 30 great years!"

Ron and his family lived for much of their lives in the Lower Mainland community of Langley. The Langley Advance News edition of January 15, 1999 ran a photo of Ron eating a McDonald's burger and this article to sum up his career.

**Marcoux bids job adieux; After 30 years with North America's top fast food chain, McDonald's top man in western Canada is saying goodbye. . . sort of**

*By Erin McKay, reporter*

The Golden Arches have given Langley's Ron Marcoux many golden opportunities. Over the past 30 years, Marcoux has travelled to locations such as Russia, Japan, Australia and France, setting up McDonald's restaurants. And as McDonald's president and CEO for western Canada, he has had the pleasure of seeing the once small chain boom into a North American institution. But now it's time to move on. Marcoux retired from his position at the end of December. However, he will stay on as a member of the board of directors in Hawaii, a job that will require him to continue to take trips to the tropical location.

"It's hard to take," laughed Marcoux, who – aside from a trip to Las Vegas – is not quite sure how he'll handle his extra spare time. Having been working since age 13, "I've never had a day of unemployment. I don't have a plan for not working," he admits. "I'm letting it roll." But one thing is for sure: he'll be around home more often. "I love Langley," said Marcoux, who lives with his wife Gail in Fraser Hills. The couple have four children and grandchildren who all live nearby.

"This is home for all of us, the whole works," he said. "We were in Langley when it was just a little place on the map." When Marcoux started the job that would grow into an incredible career, McDonald's, too, was just a little place. George Tidball, who went on to own the Keg restaurants and is currently building the Thunderbird Entertainment Centre, made Marcoux McDonald's director of real estate when there were only four or five of the restaurants in western Canada. That was in 1968. Now there are 350 McDonald's.

Marcoux was named executive vice-president in 1977, and became president and chief executive officer for McDonald's Western Canada in 1992. Marcoux takes pride in the success McDonald's had at Expo 86 and in the fact his company gives back into the community through sponsorship and Ronald McDonald houses. "People feel good having a business that helps where it can," he said.

As Ron was entering his retirement, a licensee in Squamish was creating a challenge for McDonald's. Two teenagers, unhappy with working conditions in that restaurant, took their grievances to the Canadian Auto Workers union and helped the CAW get enough members of the restaurant's crew to sign union cards to certify the CAW as bargaining agent and turn the restaurant into the only unionized McDonald's in North America. The certification came in September 1998. My role, with help from the agency's then vice-president, Rita Creurer, was to monitor what was taking place and try to keep key news media informed of facts. We visited a hotel where the CAW met with Squamish restaurant crew, were able to see how many were involved and then to talk with media from an informed position, as well as to report back to executives dealing with the issue. The two crew members who launched the effort to bring the union in said their action resulted in many improvements to working conditions, even though no contract was ever negotiated. By July, 1999, enough members of the crew had made requests to the B.C. Labour Relations Board to get a decertification vote scheduled for July 2, 1999, and the CAW was voted out.

My assignment with McDonald's came to an end soon after Marcoux's retirement. The Western Region administration hired its own inside public and media relations manager so our help wasn't required. My personal association with Ron continued for several years, however.

For a few years, we took part in the monthly tournaments of the Fraser Valley Seniors Golf Association, playing seven different courses over a seven-month season. In between, he and I often met for lunches where we "solved" no end of political problems and shared views on current events, including changes taking place at McDonald's.

Occasionally, Jack Pettitt, one of Ron's long-time McDonald's vice-presidents and then a franchisee, joined us, as did Ken Bathurst, who headed Human Resources for McDonald's for much of Ron's reign. Those fun days came to an end in 2017 as Ron's dementia challenges sent him into full-time care in a Langley residence, although Pettitt, Bathurst and I joined Ron at his residences several times including a visit in March, 2019.

## 42

## TUNNEL VISION AND A WARM RELATIONSHIP WITH HANS BENTZEN

In 1993, a voice from the past called me. Virginia O'Brien, by then Virginia Bentzen, widow of Mickey O'Brien and now wife of engineer Hans Bentzen, the man responsible for the construction and installation of what became the George Massey Tunnel carrying four lanes of traffic beneath the Fraser River between Richmond and Delta.

Virginia asked if I could meet Hans and talk about buying a full-page ad in The Sun to see if he could get some attention from the NDP government in Victoria for a Burrard Inlet crossing he was proposing. I met with them and when I heard the story, I suggested we apply the funds instead to a media relations program because the proposal was, in my assessment, newsworthy.

Bentzen, with Kurt Helin, an engineer who had worked with Hans on the Deas Island (Massey) tunnel in the early 1960s, had developed plans to use the same building technique to cross Burrard Inlet from Vancouver to the North Shore. A pamphlet prepared as a part of the communications program described the idea this way:

JIM PEACOCK

**The Hans Bentzen Tunnel:**

*A self-financing, lasting transportation solution that protects Stanley Park; saves the Lions Gate Bridge.*

The Hans Bentzen option is the only Lions Gate Bridge choice which creates new wealth to pay for itself. Hans Bentzen, P. Eng., is the man who built the Massey Tunnel beneath the Fraser River in the late 1950s. Now, as a solution to traffic and other problems arising from the aging of the over-used Lions Gate Bridge, he has updated and refined a concept he first put forward in 1963 in this proposal:

A tunnel crossing of Burrard Inlet that would meet immediate demand and provide for future growth; save the Lions Gate Bridge; remove commuter traffic from the bridge, Stanley Park and the West End of Vancouver, and virtually pay for itself.

Here are key Bentzen Tunnel factors: Six lanes for vehicles, with provision to carry through traffic from Upper Levels Highway to False Creek bridges without using existing surface streets. Two rail lines for rapid transit, linked with Sky Train in Vancouver. Self-financing through real estate development on about two-thirds of a 175-acre island to be created just off Brockton Point on Burnaby Shoal using fill from tunnel trenching and other sources. Balance of the island to be a perimeter park. Constructed with no interference with existing Lions Gate Bridge traffic. Designed and built to meet modern earthquake safety codes. Designed and developed to meet environmental requirements and Municipal and Port development guidelines. Construction Period of four to five years.

This tunnel provides a long-term solution to many traffic congestion problems for North Shore municipalities and

Vancouver. It permits restoration of the Stanley Park causeway to park use and could add as much as 50 years to the life of Lions Gate Bridge. When the tunnel is complete the bridge could be refurbished for use as a pedestrian and cycle crossing.

The Bentzen crossing would follow a route from the area between Burrard and Bute streets on the South Shore, to East of Stanley Park across Burnaby Shoal and the harbour to a point near the mouth of Mackay Creek, east of the foot of Pemberton on the North Shore. There it would connect with the existing street system and the Upper Levels highway.

With imagination and creative architecture, the new island could become a Vancouver harbour landmark, just as the Opera House is in Sydney, Australia. The tunnel beneath the harbour would be built using the same basic method employed in the Massey Tunnel."

The Massey tunnel was one of the first in the world to use an immersed tube tunnel construction method. Prefabricated sections were laid on the waterway bed and joined. Bentzen had kept up the idea for three decades. The tunnel proposal of 1963 had been updated and costed at $1.2-billion, much of which Bentzen said could be recovered by building high-end residential towers on the new island.

A news release was prepared and distributed with illustrations showing route and technique and identifying potential for the tunnel to ease the bottleneck represented by the three-lane causeway through Stanley Park and over the Lions Gate Bridge. Hans was briefed in preparation for interviews with both print and broadcast media. He made an appearance on the Rafe Mair open line show on CKNW radio. He and Kurt Helin made presentations to audiences and those triggered more news coverage

JIM PEACOCK

Over the ensuing months, Hans and I met at the Hotel Vancouver's Timber Club dining room to sip a martini, discuss strategies and remember the arguments Hans encountered when building the Massey Tunnel; opponents having said that it should be two lanes, not four; Hans suggesting it should perhaps be eight lanes to accommodate future growth (in hindsight, that would have made sense). He was a most interesting man to talk with, having had a role in building major infrastructure projects around the world, including the Aswan Dam in Egypt.

Less than a month before he died in 1997 at the age of 90, shortly after the NDP government rejected all tunnel suggestions and decided instead to redeck the Lions Gate bridge, he made a final open-line appearance with Mair.

His widow, Virginia Bentzen, said some time later that Hans was disappointed no one ever built the tunnel, but he remained convinced to the end that one eventually would be built. In a letter dated October 18, 2001, Virginia wrote the Editor, The Province:

"In your final transportation series article (What would you do, Page A8, Oct. 18), you have referred to a third crossing of Burrard Inlet and to "that" tunnel which, indeed, could be in place now if governments of the day had shown some foresight. However, your report leaves out some vital information about "that" tunnel. It was proposed by my late husband, Hans Bentzen, P. Eng., who put the idea forward in 1993, and I think you owe it to your readers to let them know that this is "that" tunnel. They also may like to know that the preliminary engineering work remains available and that I will be glad to hear from the transportation authorities when they're ready to look at the idea."

As for me, I believe as I work on this in 2019 that Hans Bentzen's tunnel idea continues to have merit. Hans told me at our lunches that he was not a believer in the potential of the

Internet and the electronic age in which we now live. But his foresight on transportation infrastructure was far greater than that of the politicians we tried to convince through our communications work together. And I know at least a few residents of the North Shore continue to be aware of his proposal as a result of the media attention we attracted.

# 43

# LAURIER INSTITUTE, WALL & REDEKOP AND OTHERS OF INTEREST

There were many other clients both interesting and fun to serve. One from 1989 and into the early 1990s was The Laurier Institute. This non-profit, non-partisan organization was founded by Milton Wong and other business and community leaders to advance and disseminate knowledge concerning the economic and social implications of cultural diversity.

My day to day contact was with its Executive Director Orest Krulak and Program Director Beverly Nann. But the work brought me into contact with its Board of Directors – some of Vancouver's more prominent citizens, including lawyer Les Little, then Institute Chair, who summed up its mission in an introductory document entitled "The Challenge of Diversity":

"The diversity of Canada's population is an exciting opportunity. Nonetheless, in any changing society, tensions will arise. The Laurier Institute was born in the belief that by fostering knowledge of the opportunity cultural diversity presents it (the Institute) can assist in reducing tensions in Canadian society. I am pleased to be a part of the Institute because I believe it can make a real contribution to greater understanding of the advantages of diversity."

Others on the Board included Milton Wong, a leader in the financial field and the Chinese community; Ken Georgetti, President of the B.C. Federation of Labour; Carole Taylor, then a Vancouver City Council member; lawyer Bryan Williams; Realtor Peter Maddocks, Law Professor Maurice Copithorne; past B.C. Utilities Commission Chair Marie Taylor and Peat Marwick Thorne Partner George Battye.

The Institute's programs included research, publications, education, maintenance of data banks and support for appropriate program and activities of public and private organizations, government agencies and individuals. Even then the impact of immigration on housing in the Lower Mainland was a topic of debate. In a November 15, 1989 report on the first phase of a study it conducted into population and housing in Vancouver, the Institute reported:

"This first phase of the study of factors affecting residential real estate prices in the Greater Vancouver area identified changing age composition and changing household behavior as major forces in housing demand... The study report says that in spite of the public attention it receives, migration to the Vancouver area has an increasingly minor role in the creation of housing demand.

The study, which examined trends in housing over a period from 1951-1986... concludes: 'Regardless of the level of migration assumed... and regardless of the level of household leadership rates assumed.... it is the demographic process of the aging of the post-war baby boom into 35 to 44 age group (1986 to 1996) and then into the 45 to 54 age group (1991 to 1996) that will determine the characteristics of changes in housing demand in metropolitan Vancouver in the future.'"

In the course of my work with Bev Nann, I met many of her friends in Greater Vancouver's Chinese community, was introduced to her daughter Andrea who by then was established in Toronto as an outstanding dancer, choreographer, dance educator, and artistic director. In Toronto she incorporated Andrea Nann Dreamwalker Dance Company in 2005 and established it as a charitable organization.

In addition to preparing newsletters and doing media relations work with Bev for the Institution, I assisted Bev in publicizing Asian Heritage Month events and on occasion when Andrea visited Vancouver helped to publicize her work. Bev's many years of service to the multicultural community earned her recognition as a member of the Order of British Columbia. Involved from the start in the establishment of The Laurier Institution, she was an active participant in the organization's affairs.

She earned a B.A. BSW and M.S.W. from UBC, then worked in social services as a management consultant. She is a former executive director of the Affiliation of Multicultural Societies and Service Agencies of B.C. (AMSSA). She was involved in establishing the Pacific Immigrant Resources Society, the Burnaby Multicultural Society, and Multicultural Home-School Liaison Workers services in the Burnaby and Vancouver school districts. She is past-president of Asian Heritage Month which is celebrated annually in May. As well, she is president of the Harry and Lin Chin Foundation and a board member of Tenants Resource Advisory Centre. Over the past 30 years she has served on many local, provincial and federal advisory bodies and is an Honourary Advisory Board Alumni of Big Sisters.

Another client was Metro Vancouver, the municipal body representing 21 municipalities in B.C.'s Lower Mainland whose Board is comprised of mayors and councillors from these communities. It was then known as the Greater Vancouver Regional District (GVRD) Our job was to assist the one-person (Bud Elsie) communications department in publicizing GVRD planning programs involving public participation to develop guidelines and regulations for growth in the region, as well as creating greater public understanding of the functions carried out by the GVRD (sewage and waste water treatment; water storage, purification and distribution, regional parks infrastructure).

The work got us involved with the GVRD's incinerator in Burnaby and the operator of that waste-to-energy facility – Montenay Inc., a company founded in 1978 and based at the incinerator plant's Burnaby, B.C location on Riverbend Drive. My contact in the early part of this assignment was the late Terry Guest. He was succeeded briefly by Ken Boatright. Then Ron Richter became Montenay's Plant Manager. Jane McKenzie was Executive Assistant to Ron and she came back into my social orbit a few years later when she was hired by Pitt Meadows Golf Club as Comptroller, a post she left in 2018. Her help refreshed my memory on the foregoing Plant Manager names.

We also served Celgar Pulp Company, a part of Stone Consolidated Inc. of Montreal – a subsidiary of Chicago-based Stone Container Corporation. Celgar operated a major pulp mill on the Columbia River at Castlegar in B.C.'s West Kootenay region, then a hotbed of environmental extremists who, from my personal experience seemed to believe that they earned credibility by pounding their fingers into your chest while shouting out their arguments as loudly as possible. The louder they were, the "righter" they were seemed a common philosophy.

We worked with the company in a program to inform the community of the benefits to environment and economy from a $700 million investment in mill modernization that saw the old mill replaced in mid-1993 by the new 1,200-tonnes-per-day bleached kraft pulp mill, virtually doubling production capacity while significantly reducing environmental impact.

Media relations and preparation of Annual Reports and other information documents were our assignments with two other clients: The B.C. Securities Commission, where key contacts were the Chair, Douglas Hyndman, and the Executive Director, Dean Holley who left the Commission in 1996 to run his own financial business called Capital Market Consulting Corp.; The Vancouver Foundation, Canada's largest Community Foundation where President Richard Mulcaster and Vice-President John Binstead were key contacts, along with his Assistant Maureen Giefing, who came back into my social life when she attended the last two Advertising Old Farts luncheons, described in a separate chapter.

We worked again with Chuck Connaghan when he headed the 2000 Judicial Compensation Committee. We helped the Real Canadian Superstore ownership with media, community and City Council communications that enabled them to earn their permits to build their first two stores in Vancouver on South West Marine Drive near Main Street and South East Marine at Rupert.

Wall and Redekop, a real estate sales and development company established by Peter Wall and Peter Redekop, brought us in touch with Robert Lee whose real estate sales propelled him into multi-millionaire status while building Wall and Redekop's reputation and income; and with B.C. Lions quarterback Joe Kapp who brought his celebrity name to a lounge in a Broadway Hotel opened by Wall & Redekop. Lee later became Chancellor of the University of B.C. and a noted philanthropist, providing financial support to many community institutions. My last personal meeting with him came in 2009 at graduation ceremonies for our granddaughter Keegan Balcom at Mulgrave School in West Vancouver. Lee's granddaughter was in the same graduating class.

One of the wildest client rides in my memory bank was with the Bank of B.C. when Edgar Kaiser, Jr. was in command and trying to expand into Saskatchewan. Paul Manning and Cindy Grauer were also on Kaiser's team at the time, a time of private jet travel to Regina and elsewhere; a time of long, sometimes hard hours, followed by watching a football game from Kaiser's suite at B.C. Place.

There was much less excitement – and pressure – in work for the B.C. Building Safety Advisory Council established by the Minister of Municipal Affairs with support from more than a dozen organizations involved in building – from engineers, architects, owners, managers and professional builders to contractor associations and municipalities. The Council gave advice to the Minister and promoted "Building Safety Week" to encourage both building safety and an understanding of the building permitting process. We researched and prepared documents for use in pursuit of those objectives.

Jake Bergen was a developer who also was a friend of Rita Creurer. She and I helped to publicize his development of the Great Pacific Forum in Delta, at the South End of the Alex Fraser Bridge, and staged its official opening. It became Planet Ice Delta and is the home of the Delta Hockey Academy, a four-rink high performance hockey training centre.

In my experience, it was a rare occasion when a consultant fired a client, but I did that once – with a successful businessman who took it upon himself to do some "media relations work" without asking my advice. He chased a radio news reporter off a property while he carried a two-by-four as a weapon – an intolerable action which prompted my immediate withdrawal from all work with him, then and for the future. So far as I know, he continued to succeed financially. But not with my help.

# 44

## COMMUNITY CENTRE ASSOCIATION VOLUNTEERS A FUN ASSIGNMENT

In 1999, as the City of Vancouver prepared for a civic election that included a vote on whether to approve borrowing for capital investment to upgrade and expand facilities of its many community centres, Kathleen Bigsby called our agency to discuss a communications assignment. A meeting at the Sunset community centre in south Vancouver led to three election campaigns of work with the Presidents Council of the Vancouver Community Centre Associations, plus a brief stint with the Trout Lake Community Association to help them get a new ice rink.

Rita Creurer worked with me throughout the activities of the three main campaigns and her talents at computer preparation for newsletters and other communications documents were put to good use as we helped the Presidents Council communicate with association members, with Vancouver's elected Board of Parks and its staff, with City Council members and with city voters.

Bigsby, President of the Kerrisdale Community Association, for several years, led the Presidents Council throughout our three election campaign assignments. The council had been established by the associations to help them reach agreement on investment priorities and to end what appeared to be unproductive competition between East and West Side centres for available capital plan dollars. The Council also sought to get Park Board, City Council and voter approval for larger capital plans.

Vancouver was – and continues to be – unique in that it is the only B.C. city with an elected Parks Board and the only city where the volunteer associations had formal agreements with the Board for the day-to-day operation of the centres and their programs, all in conjunction with Park Board staff.

When we set out on this assignment we saw it as a one-off client; work for the 1999 election campaign and it would be over. We assisted the Presidents Council in preparing letters and materials for presentations to Board of Parks and City Council members, newsletters for association members, news releases for media, and advice and training for Presidents Council use in interviews.

Bigsby and her colleagues representing the 23 associations discussed and debated needs and won agreement on priorities to be recommended to Board of Parks and City Council. Rita and I sat in on many of these discussions and recognized the challenges these dedicated volunteers faced in coming to a consensus.

We were impressed by the dedication, passion and energy these volunteers put forward on behalf of their neighborhoods and from time to time were disappointed when there were signs that elected and staff officials sometimes didn't seem to recognize the value these people brought to the table.

Memory may miss some of the players, but records from the 2005 – and final campaign on which we worked – showed the following, in addition to Bigsby, then in an advisory role: **Pat Fenner, Chair**; Jenn McGinn, **Britannia**; Rick Evans, **Champlain Heights**; Joyce Saben, **Douglas Park**; Simon Roberts, **Dunbar**; Leanore Copeland. **False Creek;** Chris Payne, **Grandview-Trout Lake;** Rolf Teverly, **Hastings;** Margaret Law, **Kensington;** Susan Duffy, **Kerrisdale;** Keith Jacobson, **Killarney;** Robert Haines,

*Remember the Good Times*

**Kitsilano;** Paul Stewart, **Marpole-Oakridge;** Peter Royce, **Mount Pleasant;** Steve Bouchard, **Ray Cam;** Gayle Uthoff, **Renfrew;** Ann Warrender, **Riley Park;** Elizabeth Snow, **Roundhouse;** Rick Archambault, **Strathcona;** Ken Thompson, **Sunset;** Massimo Rossetti, **Thunderbird;** Brent Granby, **West End-Coal Harbour;** James Gill, **West Point Grey.**

The Trout Lake assignment came from Chris Payne and took place as Vancouver was gearing up for the 2010 Winter Olympic Games. The Grandview (Trout Lake) association was in dire need of a replacement for its ice rink. The Association, with a central location on Vancouver's East Side believed it should be considered as a venue for a hockey practice arena the city was to provide for the 2010 Games.

We discussed strategies, chose a public communications process to focus attention on the location's potential rather than try to go head-to-head in competition with other sites under consideration, and staged a public meeting on Saturday, Feb. 12, 2004 at the community centre.

City and Parks Board representatives, both elected and staff took part, and media attention was focused on what Chris Payne described as the potential the facility would provide for building community fitness and spirit.

The "Legacy Forum – Trout Lake's Future" was held at the Trout Lake Community Centre, starting at 2 p.m. and was followed by a "free skate" opportunity in the centre's aging ice arena. In addition to focusing on Payne's communication goal, the event provided the community with an outline of plans and an invitation to submit ideas for community-building activities and programs related to the possibility that Trout Lake would be selected as the site for the 2010 hockey practice facility.

The Legacy Forum also sought to:

- build greater community awareness of the plan for the Olympic hockey practice facility that was part of the City of Vancouver commitment to the 2010 Games;

- build awareness of the process involved in the preparation of the 2006 – 2008 Capital Plan that went before city voters in November 2005 for approval of funding of parks and recreation facilities, including the arena; and to
- create a foundation upon which Trout Lake Community Centre could develop events and programs that would enhance community spirit and physical fitness, now and in the future.

The Vancouver bid to host the 2010 Games included a commitment by the City to create a hockey practice arena at either the Trout Lake or the Killarney Community Centre, with construction to start by September 2007 and be completed by August 2008. The choice of site was to be made by the Vancouver Board of Parks and Recreation. Budget provisions for the facility totalled $5 million – half to be paid by the City and the other half to be shared by the governments of British Columbia and Canada.

Payne said: "Ideally, from our perspective, the 2006 – 2008 Capital Plan would include funding for renovation of the arena facilities at both Trout Lake and Killarney and, in light of its accessibility via public transit and its proximity to downtown Vancouver and various 2010 sites, including the Olympic Village, Trout Lake would be designated for the practice arena. Whether or not that ideal can be accommodated, our association's Board has concluded that the very prospect of being chosen as the practice facility site presents opportunities we should pursue right now."

The Trout Lake Association and its Board won kudos from City, Parks Board and provincial and federal politicians for its positive and community-support-building approach and in the end both Trout Lake and Killarney got approval for their Arena improvements. Kate Perkins, who worked closely with us in implementing the strategy, succeeded Chis Payne as Association

President. When all of the related improvements to the Trout Lake Community Centre were completed following the Olympic Games, an official opening ceremony was held and Kate invited Jean and me to attend. In an e-mailed note dated February 19, 2012, I wrote:

> "Kate, may I say once more, thank you for the invitation to your Community Centre grand opening. It was such a pleasure to see you, to see Chris, even though his health situation is sad for everyone, to see Beth and to see so many others from the Community Association Presidents who attended your wonderful event. It was quite obvious from the audience reaction that you are much loved and appreciated by your Association members – esteem well deserved by the accomplishments that have taken place at Trout Lake largely because of your leadership and that of your closest collaborators. The arena and the rest of the Centre, so well designed and so beautifully developed to take advantage of its setting, are a super credit to all of you in the association, more so (in my opinion, at least) than to Park Board and Council which only responded because of the way you and others brought your community together. A great result that will serve many generations. I am just so pleased to think that in some small way I was of some help in that – and I keep with me very happy recollections of working with you, Chris, Beth, Harry and others those several years ago. Congratulations again, and thanks again."

On February 21, 2012, I received this reply from Kate: "Thank you so much for the lovely email. How very kind of you. Saturday was not only a highlight for our community but it was one of the best days of my life. I'd never seen our community come together in such force and with such pride. You indeed contributed to our success and we remain grateful for all your work on our behalf. It was lovely to see you and to meet your wife and daughter! I hope our paths cross again."

## 45

# PARTISAN POLITICS TO HELP RID US OF THE NDP

As a working journalist, I deliberately stayed out of partisan politics. But by the late 1990s, I was into the media and public relations part of my career and I was thoroughly fed up with the actions of the then NDP government running roughshod over British Columbians. I had seen attitudes during the short-lived Dave Barrett NDP reign that demonstrated for me at least that the NDP governed more to do things TO the electorate than to do things FOR us.

I sought out and found an opportunity to volunteer for the B.C. Liberals as a part of the constituency association supporting Christy Clark in the Port Moody – Burnaby Mountain riding which included Glenayre where we lived and voted.

In my memory of the first meeting I attended, I said I would be happy to do anything legal to help ensure the end of NDP rule. My motivation was fired by a couple of personal experiences. One occurred during the Barrett government's time when the NDP built up a $75 million health planning bureaucracy that neither added to health infrastructure nor improved health care.

Then Health Minister Dennis Cocke would not respond to phone calls or correspondence related to a Variety Club decision to raise $1 million plus towards a new outpatient clinic for the then existing and out-of-date Children's Hospital on 59th Avenue in Vancouver. In fact, the minister had a supporter named Jack Christiansen — he was a client of mine while I was at the O'Brien agency — call me to suggest the Variety Club should stay out of this whole issue. I told him I heard what he was saying but I wasn't listening! And, when the government changed in 1995, we approached the new Premier Bill Bennett and the rest is history recorded elsewhere in this accounting. The Variety Club was very much involved and a new Children's Hospital got built on Oak Street.

In that same time frame, the developers of NewPort Village in Port Moody decided to take their major investments out of B.C. to San Diego, California. For 10 years, there was a big hole in the ground above the St. James Well pub in NewPort Village. Not until the NDP was voted out of office did Bosa return to investment in the Village.

The Sinclair building, long-planned as a 22-storey high rise at 235 Guildford Way, eventually was built in time for us to move into our beautiful 21st floor penthouse suite in 2004. We lived there for 13 years before mobility issues made changes necessary. The condo was sold near the end of 2018 and the move out was completed in January 2019.

In the meantime, I became heavily involved in the constituency affairs, largely in communication roles, first for the Port Moody-Burnaby Mountain riding which elected Christy Clark in the 1996 general election and, following a riding redistribution, in Port Moody-Westwood where Christy, who served as co-chair of the May 2001 election campaign, was re-elected along with 76 other B.C. Liberals, leaving only two of the 79 legislative seats in the hands of the NDP. When Gordon Campbell named his Cabinet, Christy Clark was Minister of Education, Deputy Premier and Vice-Chair of Treasury Board.

Ann Kitching, a long-time Port Moody resident and prominent volunteer in many fields, including politics and the arts and

*Remember the Good Times*

for some years Chair of the Board of Douglas College, served as riding association president, as did Ross Murray, a Port Moody businessman. In due course, I wound up in that post, working with the likes of Kim Haakstead, who became a senior aide to Christy; Ken Milloy, Rob Boies, Michael Davis, Jeanie Trasolini, Lynne Murray, Ken Bathurst, Wendy Cooper, Gene Vickers, Hal Weinberg, Arun Garg, Gerry Shinkewski, Lola Oduwole, Adam Yoshida and, of course, Christy's then husband Mark Marissen and brother Bruce.

Documents in my files show I was media and communications committee chair for several years and in 2003 was persuaded to become Riding Association president. The activities I undertook on behalf of the constituency association included communication to keep the riding association's executive members, the riding membership and community opinion leaders up to date with riding and MLA happenings. They also included publicizing Christy's participation in community events, among them a brunch with the MLA, her attendance at Golden Spike Days in Port Moody; B.C. Day picnics and regular fund-raising events.

During a couple of the B.C. Day Picnics, the CP Rail tracks were employed to take riders aboard historic rail cars between the Port Moody Recreation Centre area and the picnic site: Old Orchard Beach Park. Following the last of the train involvements, Christy sent me this personal note: "Dear Jim, This year's BC Day Picnic was the best in our seven-year history. I want to thank you for taking the time out of your provincial holiday to help organize what turned out to be a memorable community event. Without your help and hard work, our picnic would not have been such a great success."

In August, 2001 Christy Clark gave birth to her son, Hamish Michael Marissen-Clark and about that time she was named Minister of Children and Family Development. It was roughly two years after that, on Wednesday September 15, 2004 — while I was serving as the 2003-04 constituency association president and

JIM PEACOCK

preparing for a September 16, 2004 annual general meeting — I received a phone call asking if she could come see me. We'd been in our new home in NewPort Village little more than a month. She dropped in, we sat at the dining room table and talked.

Premier Campbell was on a trip to Toronto. Christy knew our riding AGM was in the immediate offing and, having decided she would not seek re-election in the next provincial election, she had to make this known before and during the AGM. She had told her husband, Mark, but no one else when she arrived at our home. She said her motivation was a need to spend more time being a mother to Hamish, a point emphasized in the statements she subsequently made publicly.

I was taken aback, not really having expected her decision, but accepted it; suggested her motivation would be credible and wished her luck in her future. She subsequently reached the Premier by phone to advise him; went to Victoria the following morning to meet with the Press Gallery, then flew back to attend the AGM. Seldom has any constituency association AGM attracted so much media attention as that one did.

In a prepared statement issued at that meeting, Christy Clark said:

"I have made a difficult decision. Difficult because I love politics. I love the people I work with, the issues I work on, and the constituents I work for. I have decided, though, that it is time to make a change. This morning I had a conversation with the Premier and told him that I do not intend to run again in the next provincial election. . . .

"My reasons for this are deeply personal but not private. Just over three years ago my son was born. He changed my life so profoundly that I cannot remember what life was like before. My husband and I have worked hard to balance busy public lives with our busy family life. We've been successful in many ways. Our son is thriving and happy and our professional lives have been fulfilling. But I have concluded that what is best for me now is to shift the balance between my family and my professional life and give more of myself to my family.

"I am proud that our government has put B.C. back on a sound financial footing and British Columbians can look forward to the difficult but ultimately pleasant experience of deciding how to spend surpluses instead of worrying about not having enough to leave our kids an inheritance."

She covered a number of other matters, including a thank you to the Premier for his faith in her and added:

What's next for me? I will continue to work hard for my constituents, the people of Port Moody-Westwood until May 27, 2005. As I make that promise, I also want to thank them for their trust and support over the past eight years. I was thrilled to be elected to serve my community in 1996 and I was very deeply honoured to be re-elected to continue to serve in 2001. Unless you have put your name on a ballot, campaigned door to door, and then waited nervously for the judgement of voters, it is impossible to describe the incredible emotional power of that experience.

"It takes courage to put your fate into the hands of others. I am blessed to have been in the hands of thousands of friends, neighbours and citizens in my community. And behind any electoral success you need a team. Quite simply, I have the best – the best riding association, the best campaign team, the best staff, and the best group of volunteers.

"I cannot thank them enough for the thousands of hours they have devoted to our party and me. To them I say: You believed in me and I hope you know how much I believe in you. My riding is strong and whoever succeeds me is a very lucky person. Eight years doesn't really feel like a long time but it sure has been a good time."

My year as Riding President ended a few months later. David Bassett was persuaded to take on that job. Iain Black, who lived on Heritage Mountain in Port Moody was persuaded to become the B.C. Liberal candidate in the riding for the 2005 election and became the MLA. I worked with the riding association to help get Iain elected.

As the years passed and Gordon Campbell resigned the party leadership, Christy returned to politics. She'd become a successful open-line radio show host on CKNW where she could influence the community in discussions of a wide variety of public issues, without having to go through election campaigns and take the abuse that can come to all those who serve in elected capacity. When she was considering whether to seek to succeed Campbell as the party leader, I used all of those points in a note I sent to her personal e-mail address trying to convince her not to give up what she had. History shows she didn't listen to me! Instead she went on to win the leadership, become Premier and then, on May 14, 2013 surprise, surprise! The punsters forecast an Adrian Dix-led NDP victory.

In a letter I sent to the Tri-City News during the 2013 campaign, I cited some of the issues noted above and concluded: "We as voters should not soon forget what earlier NDP governments have done TO us rather than FOR us. I certainly intend to keep those experiences in mind through May 2013."

Apparently a lot of other voters shared that sentiment, and when all the counting was done, Christy Clark led a majority B.C. Liberal government. Her Party won the most seats in the 2017 provincial election but fell short of a majority and her government was defeated in a confidence vote when three Green Party MLAs hooked up in a deal with the NDP.

## 46

## VOLUNTEERING TO PROMOTE THE ARTS LED TO FRIENDSHIP IN JAPAN

For several years, when the Port Moody Centre for the Arts staged an annual Arts Festival, I worked with the centre's leaders and staff to publicize various events scheduled for the centre, the Inlet Theatre (in city hall) and at other venues. Two of the leaders were Ann Kitching and Lynne Murray, both dedicated, hard-working people who made major contributions to the city's arts and political environments.

Marketing students from Douglas College were recruited to work with me in the media relations activities – and one of those students was Teiko Oba, who came to Vancouver from Japan. She returned to Japan after graduation but we stayed in touch and, when Jean and I stopped in Osaka during a Holland America Cruise, she came to the dock to meet us and joined us for dinner.

She shared her news about working with the Canadian government's Trade office in Osaka and on the return walk to our ship snapped a photo of us standing beside a giant ferris wheel.

*Teiko Oba with Barb Wood and Jim; Barb did painting on the umbrella*

I had introduced Teiko to artist Barb Wood in Vancouver and the two of them met again in Japan when Barb accompanied a City of Burnaby delegation on an exchange visit with a sister city there. Barb had prepared special drawings and assisted in presenting them to their hosts.

On December 20, 2018 I received this message from Teiko, whose title now is Trade Commissioner: "Season's Greetings from the Canadian Government Trade in OSAKA. The message celebrated 90 years of Canada-Japan trade – and it prompted this e-mail exchange.

*From me;*

Teiko, so nice to receive your greetings from Osaka. I often think of you and our very pleasant meeting in Osaka when Jean and I visited there on our cruise in 2006. Unfortunately, I have to advise that we lost Jean on September 19 this year, just four days short of her 89th birthday. I now am residing in the Astoria Retirement Residence in Port Coquitlam, a resort-like place with meal service and all kinds of amenities and activities. If you ever travel back this way I'd love to see you. Spending Christmas with family in Vancouver. Wishing you all the very best and hope this finds you well and happy.

Jim Peacock

*Her response;*

Thank you for writing me back.

I am very sorry to hear your lost Jean-san. My deepest condolences her passing. She was very kind when I visited you in your nice condo in Port Coquitlam and we have nice memory for you and her to visit Osaka! I can't believe it was in 2006! Time flies so quickly…I am glad to hear that you live in a nice place and spend Christmas with your family. For me, I will be working today (24th, although this is our emperor's birthday-national holiday) and 27th and 28th. I will definitely let you know when I visit Vancouver. Hopefully soon!

I wish you a great Christmas and new year!

## 47

## VOLUNTEERING EXTENDED TO CROSSROADS HOSPICE

Volunteer activities extended to support for the Crossroads Hospice Society which brought to Port Moody the first free-standing hospice in the Tri-Cities-New Westminster area. Tracy Price was capital campaign chair; Ted Kuntz, was Society President and Linda Kozina was its Executive Director. As they and many others prepared to celebrate the official opening of the hospice, my contribution was preparation of materials for a special insert published in the Coquitlam NOW community newspaper that invited residents to the ceremony and open house on September 6, 2003.

The insert included this article:

For the dedicated volunteers who've turned a vision into the first free-standing hospice in the Tri-Cities-New Westminster area, there now is proof that dreams do come true. That proof is found in the Crossroads Inlet Centre Hospice being officially opened on Saturday, September 6, 2003. – almost 16 years after a Sept. 30, 1987 meeting led to formation of Crossroads Hospice Society.

With the opening of its Inlet Centre Hospice, the Crossroads Hospice Society fulfills a long-standing dream, adding a valuable resource to its range of services. This is an important addition to our range of services and one that we have dreamed of since our society was registered in 1988," says Society President Ted Kuntz. "And now it takes its place alongside services our hundreds of volunteers have delivered – and will continue to deliver – to the terminally ill and their families in our community."

The 1987 meeting brought together people interested in hospice services for the region that includes Anmore, Belcarra, Coquitlam, New Westminster, Port Coquitlam and Port Moody.

"Dr. Joe McInnis, a physician in family practice, was among the leaders of that development and the Society will recognize his contribution by dedicating a garden in his name. Dr. McInnis identified the need for palliative care in the region and noted a significantly different approach from traditional medicine. In hospice services, he saw a team approach as mandatory, using the skills of physicians, nurses, dieticians, physiotherapists, pastoral care volunteers, social workers, home care workers and hospice volunteers.

"The Crossroads Hospice Society was registered December 6, 1988 as a non-profit organization and with guidance from Dr. McInnis, Pete O'Reilly, a founder who became the Society's Hospice Services Coordinator, and Dr. Denis Boyd, clinical psychologist and grief counsellor, the society began to evolve, moving beyond palliative care in hospitals to community-based hospice care.

"The 10-bed Crossroads Inlet Centre Hospice is self-contained on the fourth floor of the Inlet Centre, between Heritage Mountain Boulevard and Noons Creek Drive on Ungless Way, near Port

Moody's Civic Centre. It has been developed through a unique public-private partnership involving housing, health and community service organizations and governments and built largely with funds raised in a still-active $2.3 million capital campaign.

"The Inlet Centre is a joint project of the Burquitlam Lions, the B.C. Women's Housing Coalition, Women in Search of Housing and Shelter, the Greater Vancouver Housing Corporation and Crossroads Hospice Society. It is designed to serve a range of people in an integrated community and was made possible with the support of federal and provincial governments and the City of Port Moody.

"In addition to the hospice, the centre has 41 units of subsidized seniors supportive housing operated by Burquitlam Lions, 23 units of mature women's subsidized supportive housing operated by the B.C. Women's Coalition and Women in Search of Housing and Shelter, and 22 units of subsidized family housing managed by Greater Vancouver Housing Corporation. Under the Canada-BC Affordable Housing Agreement, the federal government provided $4 million to the Inlet Centre and the provincial government, through BC Housing, will provide $11.7 million over 35 years in operating subsidies for the Centre's housing components.

"The Hospice is being operated by Crossroads Hospice Society and the Fraser Health Authority which is funding about $1 million of the annual operating costs. The hospice has 10 private patient rooms and provides a homelike environment with a great room for relaxing and visiting, a quiet room, rooftop gardens and a full kitchen able to provide for special family foods and meals for loved ones.

"Linda Kozina, Executive Director of the Society and manager of the Crossroads Inlet Centre Hospice, said a staff of 26 and a host of volunteers now will deliver hospice services at the new facility and through ongoing home- and hospital-based programs that serve residents among the 250,000 population of Anmore, Belcarra, Coquitlam, New Westminster, Port Coquitlam and Port Moody. Each year, this free-standing hospice, the first in the area, will serve 175 clients and their respective families and friends, a circle estimated to be more than 3000 people per year.

"The Inlet Centre Hospice complements and supplements existing health services," Kozina said. "It provides an alternative to dying in the hospital and a desirable option for many when staying in their own home is no longer possible. At the same time, Crossroads Hospice Society will continue to provide the many other services upon which it has built its outstanding reputation, including recruiting and training of volunteers and the provision of vital volunteer services delivered at home, in hospitals and other community facilities."

On at least three occasions, the hospice had very special meaning for us – three friends and neighbors spent their final days there: long-time golf partner Dennis McLennan, former Province photographer Peter Hulbert; and fellow community and political volunteer Ann Kitching.

## 48

## OCEAN CRUISING BECAME A FAVOURITE; WE DID TWENTY

Our first cruise marked Jean's 60$^{th}$ birthday. The trip was short and fun. We left Vancouver aboard Holland America's Nieuw Amsterdam September 26, 1989, sailed to Los Angeles in three days and flew back to Vancouver.

*Jean and Jim boarding for their first cruise*

One of the familiar faces aboard was that of broadcast icon Jack Webster, being paid as a keynote speaker at a conference being held aboard the ship. He had a half-hour to fill in the conference program, enjoyed the rest of the cruise and a round of golf in the Los Angeles area, then he also flew back to Vancouver. Seemed like a nice way to earn a part of his livelihood!

Over the years to 2016, we went on a total of 20 cruises; the first and the fourth were the shortest at three days each, the fourth taking place in 2002 when we sailed on the Sea Princess from Vancouver to Los Angeles, rode a bus to Las Vegas and flew home from there; Our longest began May 1, 2006 in Hong Kong and took 32 days aboard HAL's Statendam. We sailed all the way back to Vancouver with stops in Shanghai, Xinang (Beijing) and Dalian in China, Pusan in South Korea, Nagasaki, Osaka, Tokyo and the northern community of Aomori in Japan, Petroplavosk on the Kamchatka peninsula of Russia, through the Bering Sea to Dutch Harbour, Kodiak and Sitka in Alaska.

We paid a visit to the Great Wall of China, where we discovered candied ginger as a tummy-settling treat still on my diet in 2018. We dined across the road from Tiananmen Square in Beijing, and as we boarded our bus to return to our hotel, bought Olympic memorabilia from street hawkers in advance of the 2008 Beijing Summer Games. Our tour of Pusan took us to a rooftop site in a very tall building where I photographed Jean pointing to two Schnauzers (just like Stach!) looking back from a wall-mounted picture.

It was while we were docked at Osaka that we reconnected with Teiko Oba then and still in 2019 with the Canadian Trade Commission office there. We also visited the Osaka Aquarium, often billed as the world's largest, riding an elevator to the eighth – and top – floor then walking down sloping ramps to look wide-eyed through the glass walls at all of the sea life displayed in created settings depicting coral reefs from around the world. Class groups of kindergarten-aged children were touring at the same time and Jean and I often talked about how impressed we were with how polite and friendly they were.

On three occasions we travelled from Vancouver to Hawaii and return. One, aboard HAL's Zaandam left Vancouver April 22, 2007, stopped in Seattle on the way and took 17 days, with stops in Hilo, Kona, Honolulu and Lahaina on Maui. That was the trip on which we connected at poolside with Gar and Anne Lunney while docked at Hilo. The second also was aboard the Zaandam, leaving Vancouver April 23, 2010, on a 16-day sailing that visited Hilo, Kona, Nawiliwili on Kuai, and Honolulu.

The first trip was enhanced by an early passenger tour backstage to meet the Zaandam singers and dancers close up. Then we enjoyed their company on several occasions when the Captain hosted cocktail parties for the passengers. We felt like we knew the performers and anticipated each performance. Second trip, the back-stage tour came one night before the end of the of the cruise and had no impact on relationships during the travel time. We wrote to HAL to comment – but saw no positive response.

On April 19, 2012, we were joined by Carolyn and Dan McArdle aboard HAL's Oosterdam for a 16-night tour to Lahaina, Hilo, Honolulu and Nawililwili. We toured the big Island to see volcanos close-up and enjoyed dinner each evening with the McArdles and, thanks to Carolyn's notes, with a very pleasant couple from White Rock named Janet and Clive.

JIM PEACOCK

*Dan and Carolyn McArdle with Jim and Jean at Big Island volcano crater*

On two occasions we cruised through the Panama Canal; the first time departing from San Diego November 11, 1999 aboard the Norwegian Sea with Noreen and Norm Sherling and two of their long-time friends – Gordon and Arlene Clay, whose son Mike later became a Councillor and then two-term Mayor of Port Moody.

The trip through the canal was fascinating – but the Norwegian Line's service left much to be desired and we decided early on that we'd not travel again with that line – and we didn't. One problem we often remembered was the temperature at our first assigned dinner table. The air conditioner was not working properly and water dripped from above, adding to the discomfort of its cold air. Napkins were stuffed into the grill but the problem was not solved until we eventually got a new table location.

Travel consultants aboard also provided out of date information about shopping in our first Mexican port and when we questioned why we should believe them for the remaining stops on the cruise, they simply brushed us off.

Our second trip through the Canal was an entirely different story. It was a President's Cruise, with our host being Cruise Connections President Sanjay Goel, whose agency had signed up some 250 passengers for this trip aboard the HAL ship Amsterdam. We flew to Toronto, then to Fort Lauderdale for an overnight stay at the Hilton and we partied from arrival at the Hilton for dinner, through breakfast departure to the ship; and throughout the voyage. The cruise took 16 days, from Fort Lauderdale, Florida to Vancouver with stops in Cartegena, Columbia; Puntarenas, Costa Rica; Corinto, Nicaragua; Peurto Vallarta and Cabo San Lucas, Mexico, and San Diego.

A highlight was a middle-of-the-night royal wedding-watching event in a ship theatre usually used for cooking shows. It was the live telecast of the wedding of Prince William and Kate. Sanjay booked the theatre and invited passengers in his group to join him and others there for cocktails and nibblers while watching the telecast from London. Some attendees wore pajamas! All were delighted and in a generous mood, exchanging happy thoughts throughout. I think we got to bed about 4 a.m. shipboard time, but we had all day to recover.

Another memorable cruise, aboard the HAL Noordam, started in Rome on May 27, 2001 and took us on 14 days of visits to the Capitals of Europe. We flew to Rome, stayed at a small hotel called the Lancelot, just a few blocks from the Coliseum. We met Norm and Noreen Sherling and their friends Carol and Bruce Lawson.

The Lancelot was our base while we toured the highlights of Rome. The hotel had a small dining room offering a common dinner complete with wine at a round table shared by all guests who chose to dine there. At one dinner sitting we introduced ourselves to a couple from Manchester, England, he a recently retired policeman named Shaw. When we said we were from Vancouver, he asked if we knew where Port Moody was. We said "yes" we live in Port Moody. He asked if we knew the Glenayre subdivision in Port Moody. We said "yes" we live in Glenayre. And, as it turned out we lived on Garrow Drive, the same street where his sister, Carol Shaw, a prominent Port Moody realtor, lived.

On the advice of neighbors David and Diana Finlay, we hired a guide in Rome. Alfredo Peparini was a former NBC TV correspondent who spoke fluent English and knew Rome and other areas of Italy very well. He had a comfortable van to carry the six of us and he guided us through the Vatican, took us to amazing restaurants, drove us to Pompei and along the Amalphi Coast for a spectacular dinner, then back to Rome. Alfredo recruited a friend named Attillia to help get us with all our luggage to the port of Civitavecchia from which we sailed. On the way there we stopped at one of his favourite spots for lunch – and were poured aboard late in the afternoon, saturated in fine Italian wine.

Our first port of call was Monte Carlo, which we toured right after its famous road race. Then we visited Marseille, Barcelona, Gibraltar, Lisbon, Vigo, Le Havre, Dover, Amsterdam, Oslo and Copenhagen.

Our first cruise to Alaska, aboard HAL's Westerdam, left Vancouver September 21, 1996, visited Ketchikan, Juneau and Glacier Bay, then returned to Vancouver. In June 2003, we joined David and Diana Finlay and four relatives from the Hembree side of the family – Jim & Elouise Wekel and Tommy and Linda Hembree – aboard Celebrity's Mercury for another seven-day visit to Alaskan waters. Of course, we sailed through Alaskan water on the last lap of our longest cruise, described above.

In May 2009, while Jean was awaiting surgery related to bladder cancer, she and I sailed for 14 days aboard HAL's Statendam to Seward, with stops in Ketchikan, Juneau, Skagway and Haines and a train-bus trip from Seward in to Anchorage. We enjoyed that trip so much we thought we'd try it again, but the second time was our last attempt at cruising. We left Vancouver May 29 and returned June 12, 2016. Jean had to use a wheelchair to get around; we had a signature suite so-called wheelchair accessible.

We had a bad experience with the suite. It was situated as far from dining areas as was possible. We got off to a bad start the first night when Jean rolled out of a single bed. The suite had a slivery ramp to its balcony that resulted in an injury to my right foot that I had to have onboard medical staff attend to. We didn't attempt to make the trip to Anchorage. Our meals were good and the dining room service was excellent but the whole experience convinced us we were beyond the stage of being able to enjoy cruising.

We had a much more positive, though a bit odd experience two years before that when Kerry treated Ginny, Jean and me to an 11-night cruise aboard the luxury Silver Seas Shadow. I say odd because we weren't accustomed to having our own butler. We had a beautiful suite, with sitting room, bedroom and two bathrooms. There were steps up to the bathrooms and that posed a problem for Jean and her then use of a walker. The walker was too wide for the doorways, so she needed help to fold it a little each time she entered a bathroom. Inconvenient, but acceptable, still we didn't really know how to take advantage of the butler services. We survived it all, however. And had much fun on two side trips.

JIM PEACOCK

*Family rode helicopter to glaciers during Juneau cruise stop; L to R, Kerry, Jim, Jean in the chopper, Ginny*

During our stop at Juneau, we took a helicopter flight over five or six glaciers, landed on one where Kerry, Ginny and I went walking and where Jean stayed aboard the chopper but enjoyed the excitement. We also made a day-long steam train trip up the Chilcotin pass on the White Pass and Yukon railway from Skagway, Alaska. On the way back to Vancouver, we stopped in Prince Rupert and Ginny and I went ashore to dine in the restaurant at the Crest Hotel where I had stayed so often during the Western LNG project days. We also stopped in Victoria and travelled to the historic Oak Bay Hotel for an impressive lunch.

## 49

# JEAN LOVED HIGHWAY DRIVING

Woven into all of the foregoing personal and career happenings were many memorable family things. For example, our daughter Virginia's Industrial First Aid ticket took her and Jean to British Columbia's northeast Peace River region cities of Dawson Creek and Fort St. John, Ginny to work on remote oil drilling rigs, Jean driving from Vancouver to visit Ginny. The experience convinced Ginny to return to school to get her degree in Mechanical Engineering. It satisfied Jean's yen for highway driving and staying in touch with Ginny.

Jean had an adventurous spirit when it came to travel. She loved highway driving. When Peggi spent a semester at the University of San Diego, attracted there by a handsome young swimmer named Todd Schopp, Jean drove herself to California, stopping in the Sacramento area to visit her grade school friend Peggy Cawsey.

Peggy, for whom Peggi was named, had married Stuart Matheson and moved with him to the California capital where he managed a Bank of America branch. We made a couple of similar trips together, one to get Peggi to San Diego, with a stop to visit

Todd's family in the San Francisco suburb of Sausolito, and another to bring her back to Vancouver. On one of those trips, I was able to play the fabled Torrey Pines golf course, an experience made more memorable because someone stole a souvenir towel off my golf bag while I was registering in the pro shop.

Few things gave Jean more pleasure than the bright red 1986 Nissan Pulsar hard-top convertible sports car the family presented to her at a dinner celebrating her 58$^{th}$ birthday at the Pan Pacific Hotel in September 1987 after her survival of her fight with cancer. Few things in her life were more disappointing to her than having to give up driving when macular degeneration so impaired her vision that she was declared legally blind and lost her driver's licence. She drove that Pulsar to Calgary. She drove me in it through the Interior of B,C. And she drove it to San Francisco after the Mathesons had moved to Mountain View, south of San Francisco, when Stuart was transferred by the bank.

When her Father Elvin Hembree died, Jean didn't hesitate to load Peggi and Kerry into the family car and drive to Calgary to be with her Mom, Lottie. Ginny, then 7 and in school, stayed home with me, with plans to meet up with the rest of the family in the Okanagan on their return from Calgary. On that trip, somewhere near Sicamous, a latch came unhooked and the hood crashed up over the windshield. Fortunately, no one was hurt. Jean took a hammer from the trunk and bashed the hood back into place well enough to drive south to Vernon and then Kelowna where Ginny and I met them.

When Ginny and Lance, then living in Edmonton, became parents for the first time with the birth of son Bryce on April 23, 1990, Jean loaded a charming wooden cradle we'd purchased in anticipation of becoming grandparents, drove to Calgary, went shopping at the Woodward's store with my brother Jack's wife, Bunny, filled the car with baby stuff, then hied herself off through an April snowfall to Edmonton. Ginny remembers getting baby clothes, diapers and other goodies. "There was no better place to shop for baby things than Woodward's," she recalls.

Jean was thrilled to take a Helijet flight from Vancouver to Victoria for her first helicopter ride during a time when the service was young and I was working with founder Danny Sitnam on communications programs to help the new enterprise get established. She was less comfortable, but excited nonetheless flying with my brother Jack in the pilot's seat, Bunny beside him, and Jean and I snugly in the two rear seats of a single-engine aircraft in which we flew from Oklahoma City to Calgary with fueling stops in Kansas City, Great Falls and Lethbridge. That came after she and I had attended a GTE public relations conference in Dallas while I was Public Affairs Director at B.C.Tel, in which GTE had an ownership position.

We travelled by train from Fort Worth, Texas to Oklahoma City to meet Jack and Bunny, a memory refreshed when they came with daughter Nola to Port Moody to attend the October 13, 2018 Celebration of Jean's life. Jack recalled a dinner at a restaurant called Molly Murphy's House of Fine Repute, many of whose staff were young actors in costume who deliberately and in a fun if sometimes embarrassing way abused the customer.

Jean had another interesting flight several years later, after I joined George MacFarlane in the agency he started. It took her to St. John's, Newfoundland for about two hours. A major client was Daon Developments, a real estate giant that built, among many office towers, Park Place on Burrard Street and 999 West Hastings, two of the finest office addresses in Vancouver. On one occasion, Daon was involved in a deal which federal law required the company to publish certain information in a daily newspaper in each of the provincial capital cities.

We had prepared a full-page ad containing the required information and had to get reproduction proofs delivered to the newspapers to meet a strict deadline. It was before the electronic age of the Internet when the material could have been distributed in a few minutes. And neither the client nor our agency was prepared to risk courier service. So we sent several couriers out with the repros. I stayed in Vancouver to monitor developments. Jean flew with George MacFarlane to Toronto, then they headed in different directions to cover the Atlantic provinces, with Jean's destination being St. John's. Her flight landed, she delivered the material and I telephoned the newspaper to cancel the order because the deal came apart at the last minute. Memory fails me on the specific details. But when that episode was done, I flew to Toronto to meet Jean and do some shopping.

She enjoyed her second helicopter flight even more than the first, this one carrying her, me, Ginny and Kerry over several glaciers and landing on one during an Alaskan cruise aboard the Silver Seas Shadow during the ship's visit to Juneau. She had to use a wheelchair for mobility by then and found it fascinating how the helicopter operators were able to use a special ramp to ease her entry and exit from the chopper. In her typical fashion, she learned more about our female pilot, including tales of piloting choppers on Grand Canyon tours, than most people would ever find out.

Jean had a great sense of humour and it led to some interesting photos. Here are a few:

*with Stach.*

*Remember the Good Times*

*in Pusan, Korea with a couple of Stachs.*

*Clowning in front of a special formal-night backdrop during a Cruise.*

JIM PEACOCK

*Making like a sea lion on a Galapogos beach*

*Checking out a giant Galapogos turtle*

## 50

# A DRAMATIC TURN IN FAMILY LIFE

Our family life took a dramatic turn following a visit Jean and I made to Edmonton to attend the Nov. 18, 1984 Grey Cup Game, played in bitter cold and won 47-17 by Winnipeg Blue Bombers over Hamilton Tiger-Cats in Commonwealth Stadium. We watched from end-zone seats.

On our return to Vancouver, the lump Jean had discovered in one breast turned out to be cancerous. The story was one of success but with many difficult health effects. Surgery was performed by two medical acquaintances, plastic surgeon Dr. Douglas Courtemanche, and the late Dr. Graham Clay.

After the first mastectomy, chemotherapy and radiation treatments contributed to heart problems that continued throughout Jean's life. Her courage in fighting back prompted daughter Peggi to write the following article in 1999:

*By Peggi Peacock*

My Mom is my hero, not because she makes the best chocolate chip cookies this side of heaven or because she accepts collect calls any time of day or night from anywhere on the planet. Jean

## JIM PEACOCK

Peacock is my hero because the second time doctors told her she had cancer she said "no thanks" and cured herself.

She might not see it this way. She claims she had excellent support from her doctors at Vancouver General Hospital, the B.C. Cancer Agency, a very close circle of friends and, of course, her family. Sure, I suppose we helped in some ways but we couldn't if she wasn't determined to help herself.

My Mom knew she had breast cancer before she went to the doctor. She and Dad were at the 1984 Grey Cup in Edmonton. It was nipple-stiffening cold. One of hers was iced up like a popsicle. The other was lifeless, unaware of the minus 20-degree temperature in the outdoor stadium. There was obviously a problem. She'd found a lump weeks earlier but it could no longer be ignored.

"I was in my third year at Simon Fraser University (SFU) and I spent most of my time in the pool. The swim team trained four hours a day, five or six days a week. Swimming was pretty much my life. At least until that night. I came home from workout and saw my sister's black Honda in the driveway. It was not an unusual sight but she wasn't supposed to be there that night. Kerry's eyes were fixed on a jade loon lifelessly floating on the oak coffee table. Dad fidgeted then softly said, 'Listen." I knew something bad was happening. He always starts the real serious talks with that word. And where was Mom? The house smelled empty.

"They've found a lump in your Mother's breast. She's having a biopsy tomorrow.' My chlorine-reddened eyes spilled rage onto the forest green velvet. We went to see her that night. She didn't cry. She didn't shed a tear. At least not in front of her girls. She was so brave. So strong. I expected her to pull a lipstick-stained Kleenex out of her hospital gown and wipe away my tears. It would all be better in the morning. She could fix anything. On our way home Dad and I stopped at Ricky's restaurant on Broadway. I'll never set foot in that place again. No offense to Ricky's. The food's probably quite good but to me it will forever taste like bad news wrapped in raw fear.

"A radical mastectomy was followed by intensive radiation and chemotherapy. Mom was a rock through it all. I showed up at the hospital one night straight from swimming and a quick stop at McDonald's drive-through. The wafts of chlorine and fries turned her as green as the doctor's scrubs but she didn't say a word. Ever observant, I finished my dinner in the hall.

"The only time I saw her cry was when hunks of her hair fell to the linoleum of our bathroom. Even then her sobs were veiled by hysterical laughter. We bought hats and wigs and even a turban or two. She looked beautiful in all of them and in none, her pate covered in downy fuzz. Always finding good in the bad Mom was delighted when her hair grew back a mass of salt and pepper curls.

Just before Christmas the next year she went to have a reduction of her remaining breast. "I've been walking in circles she complained. A new growth was found. It was tiny and had not spread from the original cancer. This was new. She would have to start all over. It was then that Mom said "Enough!' Mom believes there are a lot of powers in the universe and decided it was time for her to call in some backup.

The previous year I'd taken a course at SFU called Altered States of Consciousness taught by a wonderful professor, Dr. Robert Harper. My swim coaches Paul and Marg Savage told me that fear was the worst part of cancer and things we don't understand generate fear. They counseled me to learn as much as I could about cancer and cancer treatments. With Dr. Harper's help I used the course to explore altered state in the treatment of cancer. I spent the entire semester researching psychoneuroimmunology – a really long word that simply means mind over matter. The theory is the brain or mind states affect body states or, more specifically, the immune system.

Mom was fascinated with my efforts and, with a little encouraging, decided to audit the course in 1986. Part of each seminar was devoted to practicing reaching altered states through relaxation techniques. Mom would lie down on the carpeted floor with all the other students and breath slowly through her nose and out through her mouth. In his gently persuasive voice Dr. Harper led the class through the forests with gently babbling brooks to quiet places where the real world could not intrude. Mom learned to shut out the daily noise and concentrate on herself, a difficult task for a woman who had devoted her life to making others happy.

She told me she'd read a story about a little boy with a brain tumour. He used the image of a big gun and shot the tumour to bits. Later tests showed the tumour had disappeared. "If he can do that, so can I," she declared with great determination. Mom, a firm believer in the value of library cards, raced through any material she could find about applications of imaging techniques in the treatment of cancer. At the time, PacMan was a popular video game. She liked the image of the little round fellow racing round munching the yellow dots and the bad guys. Mom would lie down on her bed, breathing deeply and take herself to a quiet place. Her internal PacMan would race around her body eating every cancer cell in sight.

She refused chemotherapy and radiation the second time around. She told her doctors she was trying something else. With the spread of the cancer to her lymph nodes the doctors would have preferred an aggressive clinical approach but my Mom left no room for argument. Those doctors now refer to her as a miracle patient. The cancer is gone but Mom continues to monitor her body. She has, however, switched to a less aggressive image. Today Mom has rainbows and butterflies that patrol her system.

My Mom turned 70 this year. She finished chasing cancer out of her body. Now she chases my baby girl Hallie around instead. There was a time when she thought she wouldn't live to see her grandchildren. Now, she is their hero, too.

## 51

# NEW FAMILY HEALTH CHALLENGES AND A FATEFUL 2018 FRIDAY

As it turned out some 25 years later, cancer re-entered Jean's body. In particular, her bladder. After many treatments and problems related to it, on the advice of Dr. John Warner, a urologist, she had her bladder and many other internal organs removed on June 9, 2009 at Burnaby General Hospital.

Before the surgery, to help ease tensions while we waited, we booked a trip aboard Holland America's Statendam cruising from Vancouver to Seward, Alaska and back, one of 19 cruises we sailed on over the years from September 1989 to May 2016.

After the surgery and release from hospital, we spent a year working with home-care nurses and other medical experts to help Jean recover from effects of an infection that kept her in Burnaby General 17 days longer than anticipated. The infection re-opened the incision in her abdomen and by the time it healed, with help of a VAC bandage system, she had developed a huge hernia she carried for the rest of her years.

Mobility issues increased following all of that and we often talked about how fortunate it was that in 2004 we had moved into the Sinclair condominium tower in NewPort Village in Port

Moody's Inlet Centre when we did. Suite 2102, two bedrooms and den, two bathrooms, in-suite laundry, compact kitchen, living and dining room space, all in a 1,525-square foot layout with decks looking east and west.

We equipped the walk-in shower with safety bars, the bedroom with a pole to assist with transfers between a wheelchair and a hospital bed, and we employed outside agencies to provide in-home care several days a week. That enabled Jean and I to live there together for 13 years.

More health complications came in 2017 and several months of that year were spent in ERH. By December 2017, with macular degeneration resulting in her being declared legally blind and her physical mobility becoming increasingly restricted, she moved December 6, 2017 into residential care at Park Place Shaughnessy Care Centre in Port Coquitlam.

With the help of all three daughters, sons-in-law and grandchildren, we were able to make her room attractive, comforting and homey, walls painted in the same basic colours as the condominium, her favourite paintings on the walls along with other artwork and family photos. A few of her caregivers there were equally satisfying.

However, on a fateful Friday, September 14, 2018, our daughter Peggi and I decided I should call 911, get an ambulance to Shaughnessy and take Jean to Eagle Ridge Hospital in Port Moody to have serious breathing problems addressed. Ironically, as it turned out, the medical director of the Park Place Shaughnessy Care Centre, where Jean lived from December 6, 2017, had called me to say he wanted to write requisitions for x-ray and ultrasound tests and send Jean to ERH to have them done. He explained it was not an emergency but that Jean had asked him to confirm with me her agreement to have this done. I agreed, then made my way to Jean's room expecting her to be transported to ERH that day. Turned out that was not to be.

When I learned the tests were scheduled four days later – Tuesday, September 18 — I asked staff to call for an ambulance.

Staff went to the site manager for direction. I dialed 911 on my cell phone; two firefighter paramedics showed up in minutes; three more paramedics came with the ambulance. When they listened with stethoscopes to Jean's breathing, they said it seemed like fluid on the lungs was the problem.

The hospital's tests confirmed that diagnosis. A tapping procedure to drain fluid was proposed. But it was Friday afternoon; Eagle Ridge Hospital staffing changed for the weekend, the doctor who might perform the procedure was gone until Monday, the doctor in charge rightfully decided some less aggressive treatment would serve through to Monday when a C.T. Scan showed one pocket over the right lung with a large amount of fluid.

Drainage was scheduled for 11 a.m. Tuesday – at the Royal Columbian Hospital about 30 minutes away in New Westminster. The procedure was done, removing one litre of fluid. Jean then was returned to ERH, survived more blood testing and an x-ray that confirmed still more fluid existed. On Wednesday morning, daughter Peggi, on breakfast time patrol, found her Mother a little cranky but apparently feeling pretty good. Medical staff agreed with that assessment. Peggi went home. I joined Jean in her hospital room.

Dr. Travis Musgrave requested insertion of an IV for delivery of medications to help with more fluid drainage. The IV was inserted in Jean's left foot because other options had been exhausted. The nurse took blood pressure readings before medicine delivery and found readings were low. She advised the doctor, who advised me of risks delivering medicine when blood pressure was that low.

I sent a text message to Peggi. She returned to ERH, as did her sister Virginia, along with her husband Lance. Daughter Kerry was in Philadelphia but managed to get to a place where she could call to a cell phone that enabled Jean to hear Kerry's voice and acknowledge it visibly to those in the room.

Meantime two more doctors showed up – Dr. Randy D.

Chung who had done the drainage procedure and Dr. Vineet Bhan, a partner of Jean's personal cardiologist Dr. Benjamin Leung. They checked and discussed Jean's status and spoke with us. No likelihood of a miraculous recovery of the ailing heart was the basic message.

Dr. Bhan added a comment about the relationship between Jean and Dr. Leung, saying Dr. Leung had told him how fond he was of Jean. I know that feeling was mutual because I heard the conversations during Jean's visits to his Tri-Cities Cardiology. She always asked him about his family, gave motherly advice when his father took ill, when he became engaged and when they chatted about his travels.

From her hospital bed on this day Jean said to the family members "Remember the good times" and, when Dr. Musgrave, with an amazingly warm bedside manner, invited her to choose between continued aggressive medicine to prolong things or treatment to keep her comfortable, she said clearly through the oxygen mask she was wearing "the latter and thank you for that, doctor. Don't resurrect me. I trust you completely and thank you for all you have done."

Soon after, she removed the mask from her face, refused to have it re-connected and in her inimitable self-control mode, left this world for a better place. As Peggi said in some notes to relatives and friends, "Yup, the ever-ready Momma finally ran out of batteries."

She died about 4 p.m., Wednesday, Sept. 19, 2018. That marked the end of our 66-plus years together, four days short of her 89th birthday and three months short of our 67th anniversary. There were tears. There were hugs. There was quiet. Nurses and doctors all had kind words of condolence. All of us recognized that we had to move on and I believe we shared a sense of distant relief that Jean would suffer no more – at the hands of her many, many health issues or the hands of some caregivers who didn't really know how to care enough, try as they might.

We received no explanation as to why the Shaughnessy Care

*Remember the Good Times*

Centre medical director, Dr. Eugene D'Archangelo did not send Jean to hospital on an urgent basis. Site manager Jan Taylor, who initially complained to me and Peggi about us over-riding the bookings that resulted from Dr. D'Archangelo's requisitions, sent me a card with this terse message:

> "In loving memory of Jean. May she rest in peace
>     Love : Blessing, Jan, Staff & co-residents."

Tributes that came from far and wide reminded me of a note I wrote and e-mailed to Peggi on October 24, 2016, a week after marking my 85$^{th}$ year. That note was quoted again as part of the family tribute at the celebration of Jean's life and is set out in full in the final chapter of this memoir.

In my files, I also found a copy of the May 11,1992 Province newspaper which carried a three-column photo of Jean with daughter Virginia, grandson Bryce and granddaughter Keegan, taken at a Mother's Day brunch raising funds for Grace Hospital. Under the headline "1,000 pay tribute to moms, Grace Hospital" the article read:

> "It was billed as the world's biggest Mother's Day brunch. But for Port Moody mother and grandmother Jean Peacock, it was a chance to be spoiled rotten. Peacock, 62, joined a sellout crowd of about 1,000 at the Plaza of Nations in Vancouver, where she shared brunch with her three daughters and two grandchildren. With nine-month-old granddaughter Keegan bouncing on her knee, Peacock had nothing but praise for motherhood. 'You need two bathrooms and two phone lines for all the calls, but I would have terrible regrets if I did not have those kids.'

> "Her eldest daughter, Virginia Balcom, 35, said her mother's greatest advice was 'that I can do anything I want if I only try hard enough.' Her mother 'also taught me how to cook with whatever I have in the kitchen' Balcom said.

"Another mother/grandmother at the brunch was Social Credit grande-dame Grace McCarthy. Being a mother and a politician at the same time wasn't always easy, McCarthy admitted. 'It was difficult but I had terrific support from my husband and family.' The brunch, in aid of Grace Hospital, raised an estimated $40,000. Grace is a prime maternity hospital and organizer Laurie Tetarenko said the funds are earmarked for new equipment and research. McCarthy's connection with Grace Hospital goes back a long way. On Oct. 14, 1927, she became the second child born there. 'My mother named me after the hospital,' said McCarthy, who headed home to a quiet family dinner with her children, Mary and Calvin, and three grandchildren."

## 52

## WE REMEMBERED A LIFE WELL LIVED, ESPECIALLY THE GOOD TIMES

On October 13, 2018, in the Glenayre Community Centre where we had spent many good times, our family and about 100 friends and neighbors gathered to celebrate Jean's life.

Hallie and Zoey flew home from Kingston where both are attending Queen's University and were there to support their parents, Peggi and Phil. Bryce Balcom had spent a week in Vancouver earlier supporting his parents, Virginia and Lance Balcom. Their daughter Keegan participated with presentations of "Shit my Grandma Says" recalled from travel with Jean to Las Vegas; her husband Wes helped set up technology for sound and a slide show with photos from a life well lived. Niece Karen (Hembree) and her husband Wayne Baldock; nephew Dick Hembree and wife Lynn; Niece Danielle and nephew Tony, the children of my late older brother Don, attended, Tony travelling from his Utah home. My younger brother, Jack and his wife Bunny and daughter Nola came from Calgary. Balcom family members: Jose, Marni, Devlin and Kai Robasso; Tracy and Rob Lazenby. Jean's cousin Timmy Cochlan found her way to Glenayre, not without difficulty. Anne Lunney, Gar's widow who had become a close and supportive friend of both Jean and me since our 2007 re-connection with Gar in Hilo Harbour, brought her warm wishes.

Long-time friends and neighbors from Glenayre – some now scattered to many other locations – were there: Noreen Sherling, Carolyn and Dan McArdle, Don and Lynne Monk, David and Diana Finlay; Ted and Phyllis Slinger; Marlene Campeau; Betty Wright. Cathy & Bonnie Townsend who lived across the street from us when we were in our second Glenayre house on Garrow Drive (Cathy still lived there in 2018.). Our two 21$^{st}$ floor neighbors – Simone Anand and Brigitte Boenig attended.

From my business past, Brian Ross, Darlene Poole and Ken and Lorraine Bathurst were there; Mayor Mike Clay and Councillor Diane Dilworth took time out of a busy election campaign to attend. Our long-time friend and accountant Wayne Tanaka attended.

Many friends of our daughters, including Tracy Saunders who had recently lost her own mother, and Tracy Boder and husband David Price. Kerry's long-time bank associates and good friends Richard and Lynda O'Donnell and Don Smith and his wife Phyllis Kinney; Kerry's TD Bank boss Teri Currie flew out from Toronto to provide support for her; Jean's excellent financial advisor from TD, Crystal Wong, and local TD Bank executive Mary Vellani also were among the celebrants.

So was Wilbour Kelsick of MaxFit, our family chiropractor and dear friend, who had treated Jean's physical ailments for nearly 20 years. He and Jean both claimed Jean was his surrogate mother, which Wilbour acknowledged again in remarks to the gathering about his long-standing relationship with this tough, stubborn lady who would tolerate only so much pain before telling him he needed a rest!

In the presentation, Kerry and Virginia took turns remembering the good times; Peggi and I followed with our own recollections and then a slide show brought together by Peggi with photos from the whole family and beyond depicting Jean's lifetime as wife, mother, traveller and courageous, sometimes outrageous responder to events and surroundings, the latter demonstrated by her November 2006 pose with a sea lion on a Galapogos Islands beach and another kicking up her heels earlier that year on a Dawn Princess shipboard stairway made to resemble the entrance to the ballroom of the Titanic as a backdrop for formal night photos.

## 53

# SHIT MY GRANDMOTHER SAYS

Granddaughter Keegan Balcom, with a little help from brother Bryce and cousins Hallie and Zoey, assembled over time what they called "Shit My Grandmother Says." This is the file that was displayed at our celebration of Jean's Life well lived:

Following a stroke and with broken ribs *"there's nothing wrong with me that a good kick in the ass wouldn't cure"*

---

At her 87th birthday party, she turned to Zoey: *"I'm not coming to your play unless you're naked"*

---

Grandma: *"Oh, so you're going hunting? With a gun?"* Jose: *"No, with a bow and arrow"* Grandma: *"Oh well, the animals are safe then"*

Nearing the runway, on an all-girls visit to Las Vegas when she was 83, Jean provided many additions to this "shit list".

---

When the plane pulled up at the last minute, Grandma, Ginny and Keegan were discussing various methods to encourage the pilot to share the reason for the avoided landing. Grandma said *"It's amazing what you can do with the power of a little old lady"*

---

A man on a plane taxiing to its gate in Vegas exclaimed: *"It's 37 degrees in here!"*" Grandma: *"Just take your clothes off"*

---

After arriving in Vegas airport, a young man was pushing Grandma in a wheelchair. She and the family were taken though a short cut with automatic doors to the baggage carousel, she said **"That's magic, I like magic sensors"**

---

In Vegas, Grandmother told the family that we needed to make sure to put our PJs out before going to the casino at night because who knew what sense we would have left when we got back.

---

In Vegas at the pool, Grandma started splashing Keegan and exclaimed *"It was that little kid that was splashing you!"* pointing at a young boy.

Keegan shared with Jean and the family that she was recording *'Shit my Grandma Says'*, Jean responded *"I don't say funny things at all"*

---

In Vegas, the family was concerned about Grandma wandering the enormous hotel on her own with her eyesight failing, but she made sure to let us know that she *"knows where the casino is you know"*.

---

*"I'm down playing sex in the city"* - a slot machine. Keegan was taking a note, Grandma wondered aloud *"are you doing grandma shits?"*

---

Hallie wanted a nice dress to attend the show "O" in Vegas, but Grandma informed us *"I think you could go naked to O and no one would notice, they would just think you're a diver"*

---

Discussing places we wanted to go before breakfast in Vegas, grandma asked *"The margarita place? For breakfast?"*

---

*"When I'm without grandpa, I make a lot of friends, but he gets a little cross when he has to wait for me because I'm chatting someone up"*

JIM PEACOCK

Grandma had a question for the lifeguard on duty in Vegas. Grandma: *"you have a really hard job, how many people have drowned?* Lifeguard: *"maybe 9 or so."* Grandma: *"well that's really a lot for one day!"* Lifeguard: *"oh, that wasn't just today!"*

---

Jean shared her preference for cocktails *"I just like my vodka"*

---

Talking about genes with Zoey *"you're a Hembree, it's too bad, but you are"*

---

If you don't start reading that book, I'm going to kill you now."

---

At Circo restaurant in the Bellagio *"Just look at those balls up there and amuse yourself, they look like stripped balls"*

---

She was handed a ceasar *"this is enough vegetables for my lunch!"*

---

To manager of the Circo restaurant *"I'm 83, but feel 90"*

*"Why would I want that Hallie cause you might want to put it in your hair!"*

---

Chatting with Marni and Tracey about their late mother Judy *"Did she go around checking mens' bums? Cause I do, it's one of my games!"*

---

Grandma was meeting the family at the pool, and Ginny had asked her to *"Just stand by the life guard and we'll see you."* Grandma said *"I'll tickle his toes"*. When she did find us she told us disappointedly *"It was a girl"*.

---

A group of our family was standing at the elevators in Vegas waiting for other family to head downstairs. The elevator doors opened to reveal a grumpy looking man. The doors closed. Grandmother stated *"We didn't like your face"*.

---

Out for Burgers, Grandma said to Tracey: *"I only hit you once yesterday!"* Tracey: *"No, you hit me twice! And apologized to me after each one!"*

---

Standing in an elevator, Grandma is poking Tracey in the back. *"I was reading the label on the back of your shirt with brail"* (It was a rubbery logo).

JIM PEACOCK

*"I have a new diet, it's called water and candy."*

---

Walking down the hallway holding hands with Hallie and Zoey on either side *"A rose between two thorns"*

## 54

# MOM WAS A LOT OF THINGS

The following notes sum up the tributes to Jean as the family sought to remember the good times at our celebration of her life October 13, 2018.

### Little Sister (Ginny)

- Dorothy, or Jean as we all knew her, was the youngest, by a long way. Her three brothers, Earl, David, and Lance (lovingly known as Huck) were 8, 11, and 14 years older than their baby sister
- And enjoyed keeping her entertained
- "Go drown this snake in the horse trough" … failing to mention it was a water snake. Mom told us how she spent hours poking that snake under water before the boys finally, hysterically, fessed up.
- "if you want dimples, just do this" as with the snake, Mom tried and tried .. anybody notice if she succeeded?

JIM PEACOCK

### Farm Girl (Kerry)

- Picture a pint sized Jean, shotgun to match, aiming at bottles lined up on the fence
- Or riding bareback around the farmlands
- Farm life earned her a hatred for mice .. she was 5 or 6 and a nest of mice fell from the rafters in the barn and the baby mice went down the back of her jacket

### She was a Wild Child (Ginny)

- Her teens found her hanging around with best friends Peggy and Merle
- sneaking out windows to meet boys
- parking in graveyards
- And on one occasion, this amorous parking involved a car out of gear, knocked over headstones and a mad scramble to put them back

### Fearless (Kerry)

- Other than mice, she was fearless
- From saving me from a garter snake that a young friend had tied around my neck
- To telling off the French teacher when he figured Ginny had forged a sick note
- To taking things apart and fixing them, like replacing the dryer belt with a pair of panty hose until the ordered belt arrived
- To facing down a terminal cancer diagnosis in 1985 by visualizing PacMan racing round her body eating up cancer cells, by getting a new puppy – Stach – and walking him every day and by being her incredibly stubborn self and saying "Nope. I'm busy. My girls still need me."

### Elegant and Creative (Ginny)

- She loved beautiful things – from art to clothing. She'd point out the details, dresses with tiny pleats, coats with hand stitching, lush fabrics, but she would often forgo these fineries to splurge on something one of us had fallen for - such as brown suede lace-up boots, or navy and white platform saddle shoes.

### Foodie (Kerry)

- Long before there was such a thing.
- When it was her turn to host the Gourmet Club she'd devour Gourmet magazine, and practice each recipe on us before the big night
- Always interested in what went into a recipe when we went out she regularly humored the restaurant staff to share their secrets with her
- She cooked without recipes - so we had to follow her around measuring "a handful of this" and a "pinch of that" to recreate her recipes.

### Adventurous and Outgoing (Ginny)

- Mom had an incredible zest for living
- She'd grab opportunities for adventure – traveling the world,
- filming wild rickshaw rides in Bangkok,
- figuring out how to gut a chicken in Spain, and frolicking with sea lions in the Galapagos
- She looked forward to the lively Grey Cup and New Year's parties with the Glenayre crew
- And she loved to make you laugh.

She did that so much on one trip that her granddaughters started keeping a list **"shit my grandma says"**

When you read this earlier you probably Laughed Out Loud, just like mom.

### Coach, Cheerleader, Champion (Kerry)

- She believed her girls could be anything they wanted to be, and not content to watch, she'd give fate a helping hand
- In 2008 I was working here (in Vancouver) and had a chance to go back to Toronto for an interesting role – just as she was dealing with bladder cancer. She encouraged me to go - said she'd see more of me if I lived in Toronto because when I came home I'd stay with them where while I was in town she only saw me for dinners once a week . Not true but her way of sending me off to conquer the world
- 1985, when she probably knew she had breast cancer, she cut out an article about Operation Raleigh and encouraged Peggi to apply. When Peggi was offered a spot, Mom insisted she go, despite being in the middle of treatment.
- She signed herself and Ginny up for auto repair classes at night school when the high school wouldn't let girls take shop
- Always with a touch of humor – she picked you up, dusted you off, made you laugh, and sent you back out – whether you were one of her daughters, one of her grandkids, one of her many friends or her loving husband ….

## A Loving Wife (Jim)

Before I get to some personal comments about the Amazing Jean I lived with for nearly 67 years, I want to say thank you to everyone for being here today and for the wonderful and warm support you have given me and our family. And I want to read a note I received this morning from a nephew who also married a Hembree girl. Jim Wekel of Calgary, husband of a favorite niece named Elouise, who died three years ago, is travelling in London. He sent me this note this morning.

> As you have the Celebration of Life for Aunt Jean today, I will be thinking of her. Of the weekly phone calls that Jean had with Lance (Jean's brother and Ellie's Dad). Of the phone calls with Elouise and myself. It was always a better day after talking with Aunt Jean. Of the Alaskan cruise, of your visit to the cottage, and our visits to Vancouver. I wish that I could hear more stories today of Aunt Jean but I will raise a glass or two today as I remember.

On a very personal note...

When I turned 85, we had a family birthday party...

Peggi asked me then what I thought was the most amazing thing I'd seen in 85 years. I thought about that for a couple of days and then sent Peggi an e-mail note. I'd like to read it to you:

> A couple of days ago, when your mother telephoned June Elliott in an effort to cheer her up after her latest bloodwork news, the answer became clear: Your Mother is the most amazing thing that's happened to me in my 85 years.
>
> She's supported me for 66 of those years. She brought us our three lovely daughters and is largely – no, mostly – responsible for an

*upbringing that I believe has helped all three of you succeed in life, in careers and in so many other ways they can't all be described here. She has survived for 30 years the ravages of breast cancer, survived for seven years the results of bladder cancer and surgery complications that came with it, as well as vision loss and other associated ailments. Yet throughout she has served as a sounding board and mentor for you, Ginny and Kerry and now does similar things for four grandchildren, not to mention friends like June. And she continues to have patience with me and my idiosyncrasies.*

*You Mother is absolutely amazing — and I'm still in love with her.*

Now, add two years to all of that, two often painful and always stressful years during which Jean continued to show more concern for others than for herself, I continue to believe she is the most amazing person I've ever met; the most amazing thing I've seen in 87 years – and I miss her very much.

**Mom always said she was fey...** (Peggi)

The Oxford English Dictionary provides several definitions of the word but I believe this is the one she was referring to:

**Fey ADJECTIVE**

Having supernatural powers of clairvoyance.

And just to clarify:

clair·voy·ance
*noun*
1. the supposed faculty of perceiving things or events in the future or beyond normal sensory contact.

Based on those supernatural powers, Mom said she'd be here today, somewhere.

So Momma, I hope these words meet your approval, make you smile and follow the instructions you gave us just before you left.

Some of Mom's very last words to us were **"Remember the good times."**

So that's what I'm going to do here.

Just share some snippets of being Jean's daughters

Things not captured in photos

But indelibly etched in our minds and hearts

JIM PEACOCK

## Remembering The Good Times

Warm feet pound cold hardwood
Crossing the chasm of hall
Fleeing nightmare witch
Diving in beside warm, safe Mom
Covers lifted in welcome
The chemical perfume of
bejewelled gowns
Draped in drycleaning bags
Whispering over sparkly sling backs
In a favourite hide and seek closet
Big flowered box
full of Jackie O hats
The perfect adornment
To the few classic outfits
she allowed herself

Another box
Velvet lined
full of jewels,
not fancy, but fun and festive
and free to be tried on and borrowed
Musty mix of Old books and wet carpet
The weekly trip to the library
replenishing our supply
Feeding our minds
She consumed books
like I consume chocolate,
but with even greater
gusto and joy.
Whistling kettle
Heralds hot tea
Cinnamon & sugar sprinkled
Crispy pie crust extras

*Remember the Good Times*

Saved just for you
Race home for lunches of comfort food,
home made mac cheese or
creamy scrambled eggs
and fresh baked bran muffins,
dripping with warm, melty butter
The mammoth dictionary
Sitting stoutly beside her
Flipping gossamer-thin pages
On a quest for definitions
Of new words discovered at school

Paper doilies fashioned into hearts
Stuck to red construction paper
With sticky sweet LePage's glue

Home made Valentines
Created and delivered with love
Elaborate Hawaiian Easter bonnet
fashioned from turbaned hotel towel
and frangipanis plucked from the gardens
Or shredded newspaper…if you were second in line

Sugar and eggs and creamy butter,
Swirled with vanilla
Slowly stirred with oatmeal and a
Waterfall of chocolate chips
Cookie sheets carefully lined
With rows of fork pressed batter balls
Back turned to open the oven
Middle row disappeared
Sweet taste of stolen dough
Forever on my lips
Even sweeter
Her feigned anger betrayed by fleeting dimples

JIM PEACOCK

And laughter in big brown eyes

A breath of L'Air du Temps
Swirling in her wake
Calling last minute instructions
To the babysitter
As she swished out the door

Late to the car
Packed for 2 week vacation
Delayed by Dusting
With underwear on their way to the laundry

Picking up Grandma Lottie
Accidentally in the bus zone
Inconspicuous
In the Purple station wagon
Adorned with lime green 60s flowers

Street lights come on,
race home to the safety and comfort
of a house where Mom waits

Sleepy voice
answering mandatory late night check in calls
with love and relief

Measles, mumps, chicken pox or heartbreak
tucked into sofa nest, fed chicken soup and gingerale
Allowed to watch
Endless TV
On any of the three channels

Panty hose Repair
of broken dryer

*Remember the Good Times*

until ordered belt arrived

Newspaper smudged hands
Blended scents of coffee, printers ink
Pencil shavings and eraser bits
As she deliberates over the morning crossword.
Never one that could stump her

Democracy mattered.
Home exhausted
days traipsing the city streets,
enumerating the population,
every voter registered.

House full of raucous teens
Regular supervisory laps
Collecting the troubled
For tea, sandwiches and talks
Jean's unofficial counselling sessions
Friends forever grateful

4 am phone call
From Australian stranger
"G'Day! Met your Mom at a piano bar,
She thought we'd get along
Suggested I call"
Asleep in the big bed
Furry ball of Stach
Curled between neck and shoulder
Always vigilant

"Hello? Jean's Cooking school?"
Always an answer
To kitchen emergencies
No matter what hour

## JIM PEACOCK

Or from how far the call

No matter how far we moved
Edmonton, Toronto, Hong Kong
Thailand, Vietnam
Visits from Mom
Always guaranteed

Now
A big empty hole
Being slowly filled
With memories of all the good times
And knowing we were loved well and fully

Mom was incredibly intelligent,
funny, ingenious, curious

She could have been anything,
anything she set her mind to
but she chose to be what she considered the most important thing
of all – Our Mom.

**Here's to you Mom! We will always love you.**

*family and some good times*

On our last visit to Hawaii together this family photo was taken at the Turtle Bay resort we visited. Thirteen members attended. Lisa Jorgensen later became Bryce's partner. Here, L to R, are Ginny and Lance Balcom, Hallie and Zoey Jones, Bryce Balcom, Jim, Jean (seated), Peggi and Phil Jones, Kerry, Keegan Balcom and Wes Lawrence. This Christmas-New Year's gathering at the end of 2015 reminds me of the love and support of Jean and our whole family that made it possible for me to do whatever I've done, including all that's described in these pages. I will be forever grateful, as I Remember the Good Times.

# EPILOGUE

When Jean and I moved to the West Coast in November 1958, our first daughter, Virginia, wasn't yet a year old. We found a house in Glenayre, then a new subdivision in Port Moody, about 20 km from downtown Vancouver. In time, some of our friends and neighbors there were involved in the organization that eventually resulted in the 1984 opening of the Eagle Ridge Hospital, located in our city. Our family's links with Eagle Ridge Hospital go back to its start.

Jean's personal connection included time when she was a volunteer introducing elementary school-age children to the new hospital, some of its lab equipment like microscopes, and especially its cafeteria with large soup tureen and tasty cookies. She helped the kids understand the hospital as a friendly place, not one that should frighten them when they needed to come back for medical reasons.

We have two other daughters, Kerry and Peggi, both born in hospitals in New Westminster but, like their parents, interested in and supportive of Eagle Ridge Hospital and the Foundation that raises funds to finance equipment, improvements and expansion.

Daughters, sons-in-law and grandchildren took part in

and/or sponsored participants in Wheel to Heal, the Charity Golf Classic and the Evening of Caring Gala. Some had significant roles in ERHF communications and promotion.

Peter Irving, who chaired the Foundation for several years, was a friend and one-time employee of the MacFarlane, Peacock public relations firm – and I provided volunteer help to him and Foundation staff over much of that time. That relationship gave me the opportunity to help with publicity when Alison Johansen became the Chair and Charlene Giovannetti-King became Executive Director.

Through our personal contacts with Alison, Charlene and other Foundation staff, Jean and I were aware, in 2016, that something major might be afoot in the Foundation's future fundraising efforts. We were about to celebrate our 65$^{th}$ wedding anniversary, discussed some legacy-type possibilities, decided to commit $100 for each of our years together in support of the Foundation and consulted with Charlene. We delivered a letter dated December 15, 2016, -- the day of our anniversary – stating the following:

> *Dear Charlene:*
>
> *Enclosed is a cheque for $6,500, jointly from D. Jean Peacock and James A. Peacock, a contribution we have chosen to make to mark our 65$^{th}$ wedding anniversary, Dec. 15, 2016. We understand a significant capital campaign may be in the offing to help address long-overdue upgrading and expansion of Eagle Ridge Hospital and we'd like to have this contribution become a part of that campaign when it is established. If that campaign is unduly delayed, then please apply this contribution where you feel it is needed most.*
>
> *We very much appreciate the services of the hospital and the support generated by the Foundation.*

*Remember the Good Times*

THAT DIDN'T MAKE TOO big a dent in the $5 million the Foundation subsequently committed to raise – but it was a start. Many things happened after that. Jean spent many months in the care of the wonderful medical staff of the hospital, where her life ended September 19, 2018 just four days short of her 89$^{th}$ birthday.

At our family's request the Foundation established the Jean Peacock Memorial Fund. Many friends and acquaintances contributed to this Fund – too many to mention them all here. Ultimately we set a goal of $100,000 and – as a salute to Cardiologist and friend Dr. Benjamin Leung asked that it be directed particularly to support the cardiology upgrades taking place at the hospital.

That would be very important to Jean – as it is to all of our family — because it was a member of the Foundation who introduced us to Dr. Leung, who cared so well for Jean during the last years of her life.

With strong support from our daughters and their families — Virginia (Lance Balcom), Kerry and Peggi (Phil Jones) our target was met in January 2019. As a result two ECG/Event Monitoring rooms will bear plaques identifying them in memory of Jean. The Foundation also recognized the family with presentation of its prestigious Doctor of Philanthropy designation at its June 12, 2019 Donor Recognition Dinner.

Our family hopes and believes that the hospital improvements supported by the Jean Peacock Memorial Fund will help Dr. Leung and others in his profession serve the Tri-Cities population well for years to come. If it inspires others to provide support for ERHF's Capital Campaign and other fund-raising events, that will be a bonus for everyone.